FOREWORD

The collection of "Everything Will Be Okay" travel phrasebooks published by T&P Books is designed for people traveling abroad for tourism and business. The phrasebooks contain what matters most - the essentials for basic communication. This is an indispensable set of phrases to "survive" while abroad.

This phrasebook will help you in most cases where you need to ask something, get directions, find out how much something costs, etc. It can also resolve difficult communication situations where gestures just won't help.

This book contains a lot of phrases that have been grouped according to the most relevant topics. The edition also includes a small vocabulary that contains roughly 3,000 of the most frequently used words. Another section of the phrasebook provides a gastronomical dictionary that may help you order food at a restaurant or buy groceries at the store.

Take "Everything Will Be Okay" phrasebook with you on the road and you'll have an irreplaceable traveling companion who will help you find your way out of any situation and teach you to not fear speaking with foreigners.

TABLE OF CONTENTS

T&P Books Publishing

T&P Books Publishing

PHRASEBOOK

HINDI

By Andrey Taranov

THE MOST IMPORTANT PHRASES

This phrasebook contains
the most important
phrases and questions
for basic communication
Everything you need
to survive overseas

T&P BOOKS

Phrasebook + 3000-word dictionary

English-Hindi phrasebook & topical vocabulary

By Andrey Taranov

The collection of "Everything Will Be Okay" travel phrasebooks published by T&P Books is designed for people traveling abroad for tourism and business. The phrasebooks contain what matters most - the essentials for basic communication. This is an indispensable set of phrases to "survive" while abroad.

This book also includes a small topical vocabulary that contains roughly 3,000 of the most frequently used words. Another section of the phrasebook provides a gastronomical dictionary that may help you order food at a restaurant or buy groceries at the store.

T&P Books Publishing
www.tpbooks.com

ISBN: 978-1-78616-761-3

This book is also available in E-book formats.
Please visit www.tpbooks.com or the major online bookstores.

PRONUNCIATION

Letter	Hindi example	T&P phonetic alphabet	English example

Vowels

Letter	Hindi example	T&P phonetic alphabet	English example
अ	अक्सर	[a]; [ɑ], [ə]	park; teacher
आ	आगमन	[a:]	calf, palm
इ	इनाम	[i]	shorter than in feet
ई	ईश्वर	[i], [i:]	feet, Peter
उ	उठना	[ʊ]	good, booklet
ऊ	ऊपर	[u:]	pool, room
ऋ	ऋग्वेद	[r, rʲ]	green
ए	एकता	[e:]	longer than in bell
ऐ	ऐनक	[aj]	time, white
ओ	ओला	[o:]	fall, bomb
औ	औरत	[au]	loud, powder
अं	अंजीर	[ŋ]	English, ring
अः	अ से अः	[h]	home, have
ऑ	ऑफिस	[ɒ]	cotton, pocket

Consonants

Letter	Hindi example	T&P phonetic alphabet	English example
क	कमरा	[k]	clock, kiss
ख	खिड़की	[kh]	work hard
ग	गरज	[g]	game, gold
घ	घर	[gh]	g aspirated
ङ	ङाकू	[ŋ]	English, ring
च	चक्कर	[tʃ]	church, French
छ	छात्र	[tʃh]	hitchhiker
ज	जाना	[dʒ]	joke, general
झ	झलक	[dʒ]	joke, general
ञ	विज्ञान	[ɲ]	canyon, new
ट	मटर	[t]	tourist, trip
ठ	ठेका	[th]	don't have
ड	डंडा	[d]	day, doctor
ढ	ढलान	[d]	day, doctor
ण	क्षण	[n]	retroflex nasal
त	ताकत	[t]	tourist, trip

Letter	Hindi example	T&P phonetic alphabet	English example
थ	थकना	[th]	don't have
द	दरवाज़ा	[d]	day, doctor
ध	धोना	[d]	day, doctor
न	नाई	[n]	sang, thing
प	पिता	[p]	pencil, private
फ	फल	[f]	face, food
ब	बच्चा	[b]	baby, book
भ	भाई	[b]	baby, book
म	माता	[m]	magic, milk
य	याद	[j]	yes, New York
र	रीछ	[r]	rice, radio
ल	लाल	[l]	lace, people
व	वचन	[v]	very, river
श	शिक्षक	[ʃ]	machine, shark
ष	भाषा	[ʃ]	machine, shark
स	सोना	[s]	city, boss
ह	हज़ार	[h]	home, have

Additional consonants

क़	क़लम	[q]	king, club
ख़	ख़बर	[h]	huge, hat
ड़	लड़का	[r]	rice, radio
ढ़	पढ़ना	[r]	rice, radio
ग़	ग़लती	[ɣ]	between [g] and [h]
ज़	ज़िन्दगी	[z]	zebra, please
झ़	ट्रैझ़र	[ʒ]	forge, pleasure
फ़	फ़ौज	[f]	face, food

LIST OF ABBREVIATIONS

English abbreviations

ab.	-	about
adj	-	adjective
adv	-	adverb
anim.	-	animate
as adj	-	attributive noun used as adjective
e.g.	-	for example
etc.	-	et cetera
fam.	-	familiar
fem.	-	feminine
form.	-	formal
inanim.	-	inanimate
masc.	-	masculine
math	-	mathematics
mil.	-	military
n	-	noun
pl	-	plural
pron.	-	pronoun
sb	-	somebody
sing.	-	singular
sth	-	something
v aux	-	auxiliary verb
vi	-	intransitive verb
vi, vt	-	intransitive, transitive verb
vt	-	transitive verb

Hindi abbreviations

f	-	feminine noun
f pl	-	feminine plural
m	-	masculine noun
m pl	-	masculine plural

T&P BOOKS

HINDI
PHRASEBOOK

This section contains important phrases that may come in handy in various real-life situations.
The phrasebook will help you ask for directions, clarify a price, buy tickets, and order food at a restaurant

T&P Books Publishing

PHRASEBOOK
CONTENTS

T&P Books Publishing

The bare minimum

Excuse me, ...

माफ़ कीजिएगा, ...
māf kījiega, ...

Hello.

नमस्कार।
namaskār.

Thank you.

शुक्रिया।
shukriya.

Good bye.

अलविदा।
alavida.

Yes.

हाँ।
hān.

No.

नहीं।
nahin.

I don't know.

मुझे नहीं मालूम।
mujhe nahin mālūm.

Where? | Where to? | When?

कहाँ? | कहाँ जाना है? | कब?
kahān? | kahān jāna hai? | kab?

I need ...

मुझे ... चाहिए।
mujhe ... chāhie.

I want ...

मैं ... चाहता /चाहती/ हूँ।
main ... chāhata /chāhatī/ hūn.

Do you have ...?

क्या आपके पास ... है?
kya āpake pās ... hai?

Is there a ... here?

क्या यहाँ ... है?
kya yahān ... hai?

May I ...?

क्या मैं ... सकता /सकती/ हूँ?
kya main ... sakata /sakatī/ hūn?

..., please (polite request)

..., कृपया।
..., krpaya.

I'm looking for ...

मैं ... ढूँढ रहा /रही/ हूँ।
main ... dhūnrh raha /rahī/ hūn.

restroom

शौचालय
shauchālay

ATM

एटीएम
etīem

pharmacy (drugstore)

दवा की दुकान
dava kī dukān

hospital

अस्पताल
aspatāl

police station

पुलिस थाना
pulis thāna

subway

मेट्रो
metro

taxi	टैक्सी taiksī
train station	ट्रेन स्टेशन tren steshan

My name is ...	मेरा नाम ... है। mera nām ... hai
What's your name?	आपका क्या नाम है? āpaka kya nām hai?
Could you please help me?	क्या आप मेरी मदद कर सकते /सकती/ हैं? kya āp merī madad kar sakate /sakatī/ hain?
I've got a problem.	मुझे एक परेशानी है। mujhe ek pareshānī hai.
I don't feel well.	मेरी तबियत ठीक नहीं है। merī tabiyat thīk nahin hai.
Call an ambulance!	एम्बुलेन्स बुलाओ! embulens bulao!
May I make a call?	क्या मैं एक फ़ोन कर सकता /सकती/ हूँ? kya main ek fon kar sakata /sakatī/ hūn?

I'm sorry.	मुझे माफ़ करना। mujhe māf kar do.
You're welcome.	आपका स्वागत है। āpaka svāgat hai.

I, me	मैं main
you (inform.)	तू tū
he	वह vah
she	वह vah
they (masc.)	वे ve
they (fem.)	वे ve
we	हम ham
you (pl)	तुम tum
you (sg, form.)	आप āp

ENTRANCE	प्रवेश pravesh
EXIT	निकास nikās

OUT OF ORDER	ख़राब है kharāb hai
CLOSED	बंद band
OPEN	खुला khula
FOR WOMEN	महिलाओं के लिए mahilaon ke lie
FOR MEN	पुरूषों के लिए purūshon ke lie

Questions

Where?	कहाँ? kahān?
Where to?	कहाँ जाना है? kahān jāna hai?
Where from?	कहाँ से? kahān se?
Why?	क्यों? kyon?
For what reason?	किस वजह से? kis vajah se?
When?	कब? kab?
How long?	कितना समय लगेगा? kitana samay lagega?
At what time?	कितने बजे? kitane baje?
How much?	कितना? kitana?
Do you have …?	क्या आपके पास … है? kya āpake pās … hai?
Where is …?	… कहाँ है? … kahān hai?
What time is it?	क्या बजा है? kya baja hai?
May I make a call?	क्या मैं एक फ़ोन कर सकता /सकती/ हूँ? kya main ek fon kar sakata /sakatī/ hūn?
Who's there?	कौन है? kaun hai?
Can I smoke here?	क्या मैं यहाँ सिगरेट पी सकता /सकती/ हूँ? kya main yahān sigaret pī sakata /sakatī/ hūn?
May I …?	क्या मैं … सकता /सकती/ हूँ? kya main … sakata /sakatī/ hūn?

Needs

I'd like …	मुझे ... चाहिए। mujhe ... chāhie.
I don't want …	मुझे ... नहीं चाहिए। mujhe ... nahin chāhie.
I'm thirsty.	मुझे प्यास लगी है। mujhe pyās lagī hai.
I want to sleep.	मैं सोना चाहता /चाहती/ हूँ। main sona chāhata /chāhatī/ hūn.
I want …	मैं ... चाहता /चाहती/ हूँ। main ... chāhata /chāhatī/ hūn.
to wash up	हाथ-मुँह धोना hāth-munh dhona
to brush my teeth	दाँत ब्रश करना dānt brash karana
to rest a while	कुछ समय आराम करना kuchh samay ārām karana
to change my clothes	कपड़े बदलना kapare badalana
to go back to the hotel	होटल वापस जाना hotal vāpas jāna
to buy …	... खरीदना ... kharīdana
to go to …	... जाना ... jāna
to visit …	... जाना ... jāna
to meet with …	... से मिलने जाना ... se milane jāna
to make a call	फ़ोन करना fon karana
I'm tired.	मैं थक गया /गई/ हूँ। main thak gaya /gaī/ hūn.
We are tired.	हम थक गए हैं। ham thak gae hain.
I'm cold.	मुझे सर्दी लग रही है। mujhe sardī lag rahī hai.
I'm hot.	मुझे गर्मी लग रही है। mujhe garmī lag rahī hai.
I'm OK.	मैं ठीक हूँ। main thīk hūn.

I need to make a call.

मुझे फ़ोन करना है।
mujhe fon karana hai.

I need to go to the restroom.

मुझे शौचालय जाना है।
mujhe shauchālay jāna hai.

I have to go.

मुझे जाना है।
mujhe jāna hoga.

I have to go now.

मुझे अब जाना होगा।
mujhe ab jāna hoga.

Asking for directions

Excuse me, ...	माफ़ कीजिएगा, ... māf kījiega, ...
Where is ...?	... कहाँ है? ... kahān hai?
Which way is ...?	... कहाँ पड़ेगा? ... kahān parega?
Could you help me, please?	क्या आप मेरी मदद करेंगे /करेंगी/, प्लीज़? kya āp merī madad karenge /karengī/, plīz?

I'm looking for ...	मैं ... ढूंढ रहा /रही/ हूँ main ... dhūnrh raha /rahī/ hūn.
I'm looking for the exit.	मैं बाहर निकलने का रास्ता ढूँढ रहा /रही/ हूँ main bāhar nikalane ka rāsta dhūnrh raha /rahī/ hūn.
I'm going to ...	मैं ... जा रहा /रही/ हूँ main ... ja raha /rahī/ hūn.
Am I going the right way to ...?	क्या मैं ... जाने के लिए सही रास्ते पर हूँ? kya main ... jāne ke lie sahī rāste par hūn?

Is it far?	क्या वह दूर है? kya vah dūr hai?
Can I get there on foot?	क्या मैं वहाँ पैदल जा सकता /सकती/ हूँ? kya main vahān paidal ja sakata /sakatī/ hūn?
Can you show me on the map?	क्या आप मुझे नक्शे पर दिखा सकते /सकती/ हैं? kya āp mujhe nakshe par dikha sakate /sakatī/ hain?
Show me where we are right now.	मुझे दिखाईये कि हम इस वक्त कहाँ हैं| mujhe dikhaīye ki ham is vakt kahān hain.
Here	यहाँ yahān
There	वहाँ vahān
This way	इस तरफ़ is taraf

Turn right.

दायें मुड़ें।
dāyen muren.

Turn left.

बायें मुड़ें।
bāyen muren.

first (second, third) turn

पहला (दूसरा, तीसरा) मोड़
pahala (dusara, tīsara) mor

to the right

दाईं ओर
daīn or

to the left

बाईं ओर
baīn or

Go straight ahead.

सीधे जाएं।
sīdhe jaen.

Signs

WELCOME!	स्वागत! svāgat!
ENTRANCE	प्रवेश pravesh
EXIT	निकास nikās
PUSH	पुश, धकेलिए push, dhakelie
PULL	पुल, खींचिए pul, khīnchie
OPEN	खुला khula
CLOSED	बंद band
FOR WOMEN	महिलाओं के लिए mahilaon ke lie
FOR MEN	पुरूषों के लिए purūshon ke lie
GENTLEMEN, GENTS (m)	पुरूष purūsh
WOMEN (f)	महिलाएं mahilaen
DISCOUNTS	छूट chhūt
SALE	सेल sel
FREE	मुफ्त muft
NEW!	नया! naya!
ATTENTION!	ध्यान दें! dhyān den!
NO VACANCIES	कोई कमरा खाली नहीं है koī naukarī nahin hai
RESERVED	रिज़र्वड rizarvad
ADMINISTRATION	प्रबंधन prabandhan
STAFF ONLY	केवल स्टाफ़ keval stāf

BEWARE OF THE DOG! कुत्ते से बचकर रहें!
kutte se bachakar rahen!

NO SMOKING! नो स्मोकिंग!
no smoking!

DO NOT TOUCH! हाथ न लगाएं!
hāth na lagaen!

DANGEROUS खतरनाक
khataranāk

DANGER खतरा
khatara

HIGH VOLTAGE हाई वोल्टेज
haī voltej

NO SWIMMING! स्वीमिंग की अनुमति नहीं है!
svīming kī anumati nahin hai!

OUT OF ORDER ख़राब है
kharāb hai

FLAMMABLE ज्वलनशील
jvalanashīl

FORBIDDEN मनाही
manāhī

NO TRESPASSING! प्रवेश निषेध!
yahān āne kī sakht manāhī hai!

WET PAINT गीला पेंट
gīla pent

CLOSED FOR RENOVATIONS मरम्मत के लिए बंद
marammat ke lie band

WORKS AHEAD आगे कार्य प्रगित पर है
āge kāry pragit par hai

DETOUR डीटूर
dītur

Transportation. General phrases

plane	हवाई जहाज़ havaī jahāz
train	रेलगाड़ी, ट्रेन relagārī, tren
bus	बस bas
ferry	फेरी ferī
taxi	टैक्सी taiksī
car	कार kār
schedule	शिड्यूल shidyūl
Where can I see the schedule?	मैं शिड्यूल कहां देख सकता /सकती/ हूं? main shidyūl kahān dekh sakata /sakatī/ hūn?
workdays (weekdays)	कार्यदिवस kāryadivas
weekends	सप्ताहांत saptāhānt
holidays	छुट्टियां chhuttiyān
DEPARTURE	प्रस्थान prasthān
ARRIVAL	आगमन āgaman
DELAYED	देरी derī
CANCELLED	रद्द radd
next (train, etc.)	अगला agala
first	पहला pahala
last	अंतिम antim

When is the next ...?

अगला ... कब है?
agala ... kab hai?

When is the first ...?

पहला ... कब है?
pahala ... kab hai?

When is the last ...?

अंतिम ... कब है?
antim ... kab hai?

transfer (change of trains, etc.)

ट्रेन बदलना
tren badalana

to make a transfer

ट्रेन कैसे बदलें
tren kaise badalen

Do I need to make a transfer?

क्या मुझे ट्रेन बदलनी पड़गी?
kya mujhe tren badalanī paragī?

Buying tickets

Where can I buy tickets?	मैं टिकटें कुहाँ खरीद सकता /सकती/ हूँ? main tikaten kahān kharīd sakata /sakatī/ hūn?
ticket	टिकट tikat
to buy a ticket	टिकट खरीदना tikat kharīdana
ticket price	टिकट का दाम tikat ka dām
Where to?	कहाँ जाना है? kahān jāna hai?
To what station?	कौन-से स्टेशन के लिए? kaun-se steshan ke lie?
I need ...	मुझे ... चाहिए। mujhe ... chāhie.
one ticket	एक टिकट ek tikat
two tickets	दो टिकट do tikat
three tickets	तीन टिकट tīn tikat
one-way	एक तरफ़ ek taraf
round-trip	राउंड ट्रिप raund trip
first class	फर्स्ट क्लास farst klās
second class	सेकेंड क्लास sekend klās
today	आज āj
tomorrow	कल kal
the day after tomorrow	कल के बाद वाला दिन kal ke bād vāla din
in the morning	सुबह में subah men
in the afternoon	दोपहर में dopahar men
in the evening	शाम में shām men

aisle seat

आयल सीट
āyal sīt

window seat

खिड़की वाली सीट
khirakī vālī sīt

How much?

कितना?
kitana?

Can I pay by credit card?

क्या मैं क्रेडिट कार्ड से पे कर
सकता /सकती/ हूँ?
kya main kredit kārd se pe kar
sakata /sakatī/ hūn?

Bus

bus	बस bas
intercity bus	अंतरराज्यीय बस antararājyīy bas
bus stop	बस-स्टॉप bas-stop
Where's the nearest bus stop?	सबसे करीबी बस-स्टॉप कहाँ है? sabase karībī bas-stop kahān hai?
number (bus ~, etc.)	नंबर nambar
Which bus do I take to get to ...?	... जाने के लिए कौन-सी बस लेनी होगी? ... jāne ke lie kaun-sī bas lenī hogī?
Does this bus go to ...?	क्या यह बस ... जाती है? kya yah bas ... jātī hai?
How frequent are the buses?	बसें कितनी जल्दी-जल्दी आती हैं? basen kitanī jaldī-jaldī ātī hain?
every 15 minutes	हर पंद्रह मिनट har pandrah minat
every half hour	हर आधा घंटा har ādha ghanta
every hour	हर घंटा har ghanta
several times a day	दिन में कई बार din men kaī bār
... times a day	दिन में ... बार din men ... bār
schedule	शिड्यूल shidyūl
Where can I see the schedule?	मैं शिड्यूल कहाँ देख सकता /सकती/ हूँ? main shidyūl kahān dekh sakata /sakatī/ hūn?
When is the next bus?	अगली बस कब है? agalī bas kab hai?
When is the first bus?	पहली बस कब है? pahalī bas kab hai?
When is the last bus?	आखिरी बस कब है? ākhirī bas kab hai?

stop	स्टॉप
	stop
next stop	अगला स्टॉप
	agala stop
last stop (terminus)	आखिरी स्टॉप
	ākhirī stop
Stop here, please.	रोक दें, प्लीज़।
	yahān roken, plīz.
Excuse me, this is my stop.	माफ़ कीजिएगा, यह मेरा स्टॉप है।
	māf kījiega, yah mera stop hai.

Train

train	रेलगाड़ी, ट्रेन relagāṛī, tren
suburban train	लोकल ट्रेन lokal tren
long-distance train	लंबी दूरी की ट्रेन lambī dūrī kī tren
train station	ट्रेन स्टेशन tren steshan
Excuse me, where is the exit to the platform?	माफ़ कीजिएगा, प्लेटफॉर्म से निकलने का रास्ता कहाँ है? māf kījiega, pleṭaform se nikalane ka rāsta kahān hai?
Does this train go to …?	क्या यह ट्रेन ... जाती है? kya yah tren ... jātī hai?
next train	अगली ट्रेन agalī tren
When is the next train?	अगली ट्रेन कब है? agalī tren kab hai?
Where can I see the schedule?	मैं शिड्यूल कहाँ देख सकता /सकती/ हूँ? main shidyūl kahān dekh sakata /sakatī/ hūn?
From which platform?	कौन-से प्लेटफॉर्म से? kaun-se pleṭaform se?
When does the train arrive in …?	... में ट्रेन कब पहुंचती है? ... men tren kab pahunchatī hai?
Please help me.	कृपया मेरी मदद करें। kṛpaya merī madad karen.
I'm looking for my seat.	मैं अपनी सीट ढूंढ रहा /रही/ हूँ। main apanī sīṭ dhūnṛh raha /rahī/ hūn.
We're looking for our seats.	हम अपनी सीट ढूंढ रहे हैं। ham apanī sīṭ dhūnṛh rahe hain.
My seat is taken.	मेरी सीट पर कोई और बैठा है। merī sīṭ par koī aur baitha hai.
Our seats are taken.	हमारी सीटों पर कोई और बैठा है। hamārī sīṭon par koī aur baitha hai.
I'm sorry but this is my seat.	माफ़ कीजिएगा, लेकिन यह मेरी सीट है। māf kījiega, lekin yah merī sīṭ hai.

Is this seat taken?

क्या इस सीट पर कोई बैठा है?
kya is sīt par koī baitha hai?

May I sit here?

क्या मैं यहाँ बैठ सकता
/सकती/ हूँ?
kya main yāhān baith sakata
/sakatī/ hūn?

On the train. Dialogue (No ticket)

Ticket, please.

टिकट, कृपया।
tikat, krpaya.

I don't have a ticket.

मेरे पास टिकट नहीं है।
mere pās tikat nahin hai.

I lost my ticket.

मेरा टिकट खो गया।
mera tikat kho gaya.

I forgot my ticket at home.

मैं अपना टिकट घर पर भूल
गया /गई/।
main apana tikat ghar par bhūl
gaya /gaī/.

You can buy a ticket from me.

आप मुझे एक टिकट दे दें।
āp mujhe ek tikat de den.

You will also have to pay a fine.

आपको फाइन भी भरना होगा।
āpako fain bhī bharana hoga.

Okay.

ठीक है।
thīk hai.

Where are you going?

आप कहाँ जा रहे /रही/ हैं?
āp kahān ja rahe /rahī/ hain?

I'm going to …

मैं ... जा रहा /रही/ हूँ।
main ... ja raha /rahī/ hūn.

How much? I don't understand.

कितना? मैं समझी /समझी/ नहीं।
kitana? main samajhī /samajhī/ nahin.

Write it down, please.

इसे लिख दीजिए, प्लीज़।
ise likh dījie, plīz.

Okay. Can I pay with a credit card?

ठीक है। क्या मैं क्रेडिट कार्ड से पे
कर सकता /सकती/ हूँ?
thīk hai. kya main kredit kārd se pe
kar sakata /sakatī/ hūn?

Yes, you can.

हाँ, आप कर सकते हैं।
hān, āp kar sakate hain.

Here's your receipt.

यह रही आपकी रसीद।
yah rahī āpakī rasīd.

Sorry about the fine.

फाइन के बारे में माफ़ कीजिएगा।
fain ke bāre men māf kījiega.

That's okay. It was my fault.

कोई बात नहीं। वह मेरी गलती थी।
koī bāt nahin. vah merī galatī thī.

Enjoy your trip.

अपनी यात्रा का आनंद लें।
apanī yātra ka ānand len.

Taxi

taxi	टैक्सी taiksī
taxi driver	टैक्सी चलाने वाला taiksī chalāne vāla
to catch a taxi	टैक्सी पकड़ना taiksī pakarana
taxi stand	टैक्सी स्टैंड taiksī staind
Where can I get a taxi?	मुझे टैक्सी कहां मिलेगी? mujhe taiksī kahān milegī?

to call a taxi	टैक्सी बुलाना taiksī bulāna
I need a taxi.	मुझे टैक्सी चाहिए। mujhe taiksī chāhie.
Right now.	अभी। abhī.
What is your address (location)?	आपका पता क्या है? āpaka pata kya hai?
My address is …	मेरा पता है … mera pata hai …
Your destination?	आपको कहाँ जाना है? āpako kahān jāna hai?

Excuse me, …	माफ़ कीजिएगा, … māf kījiega, …
Are you available?	क्या टैक्सी खाली है? kya taiksī khālī hai?
How much is it to get to …?	… जाने के लिए कितना लगेगा? … jāne ke lie kitana lagega?
Do you know where it is?	क्या आपको पता है वह कहाँ है? kya āpako pata hai vah kahān hai?

Airport, please.	एयरपोर्ट, प्लीज़। eyaraport, plīz.
Stop here, please.	यहाँ रोकें, प्लीज़। rok den, plīz.
It's not here.	यहाँ नहीं है। yahān nahin hai.
This is the wrong address.	यह गलत पता है। yah galat pata hai.
Turn left.	बायें मुड़ें। bāyen muren.

Turn right.	दायें मुड़ें। dāyen muren.
How much do I owe you?	मुझे आपको कितने पैसे देने हैं? mujhe āpako kitane paise dene hain?
I'd like a receipt, please.	मैं एक रसीद चाहिए, प्लीज़ा main ek rasīd chāhie, plīz.
Keep the change.	छुट्टे रख लें। chhutte rakh len.

Would you please wait for me?	क्या आप मेरा इंतज़ार /करेंगे/ करेंगी? kya āp mera intazār /karenge/ karengī?
five minutes	पाँच मिनट pānch minat
ten minutes	दस मिनट das minat
fifteen minutes	पंद्रह मिनट pandrah minat
twenty minutes	बीस मिनट bīs minat
half an hour	आधा घंटा ādhe ghante

Hotel

Hello.	नमस्कार। namaskār.
My name is …	मेरा नाम ... है mera nām ... hai
I have a reservation.	मैंने बुकिंग की थी। mainne buking kī thī.
I need …	मुझे ... चाहिए। mujhe ... chāhie.
a single room	एक सिंगल कमरा ek singal kamara
a double room	एक डबल कमरा ek dabal kamara
How much is that?	यह कितने का है? yah kitane ka hai?
That's a bit expensive.	यह थोड़ा महंगा है। yah thora mahanga hai.
Do you have anything else?	क्या आपके पास कुछ और है? kya āpake pās kuchh aur hai?
I'll take it.	मैं यह ले लूँगा /लूँगी/। main yah le lūnga /lūngī/.
I'll pay in cash.	मैं नकद दूंगा /दूँगी/। main nakad dūnga /dūngī/.
I've got a problem.	मुझे एक परेशानी है। mujhe ek pareshānī hai.
My … is broken.	मेरा ... टूटा हुआ है। mera ... tūta hua hai.
My … is out of order.	मेरा ... ख़राब है। mera ... kharāb hai.
TV	टीवी tīvī
air conditioner	एयरकंडिशनर eyarakandishanar
tap	नल nal
shower	शॉवर shovar
sink	बेसिन besin
safe	तिजोरी tijorī

door lock	दरवाज़े का ताला daravāze ka tāla
electrical outlet	सॉकेट soket
hairdryer	हेयर ड्रायर heyar drāyar

I don't have ...	... नहीं है ... nahin hai
water	पानी pānī
light	लाइट lait
electricity	बिजली bijalī

Can you give me ...?	... दे सकते /सकती/ हैं? de sakate /sakatī/ hain?
a towel	तौलिया tauliya
a blanket	कम्बल kambal
slippers	चप्पल chappal
a robe	रोब rob
shampoo	शैम्पू shaimpū
soap	साबुन sābun

I'd like to change rooms.	मुझे अपना कमरा बदलना है। mujhe apana kamara badalana hai.
I can't find my key.	मुझे चाबी नहीं मिल रही है। mujhe chābī nahin mil rahī hai.
Could you open my room, please?	क्या आप मेरा कमरा खोल सकते /सकती/ हैं? kya āp mera kamara khol sakate /sakatī/ hain?

Who's there?	कौन है? kaun hai?
Come in!	अंदर आ जाओ! andar ā jao!
Just a minute!	एक मिनट! ek minat!

Not right now, please.	अभी नहीं, प्लीज़। abhī nahin, plīz.
Come to my room, please.	कृपया मेरे कमरे में आईये। krpaya mere kamare men āīye.

I'd like to order food service.

मैं फ़ूड सर्विस ऑर्डर करना चाहता /चाहती/ हूँ।
main fūd sarvis ordar karana chāhata /chāhatī/ hūn.

My room number is …

मेरा कमरा नंबर है …
mera kamara nambar hai …

I'm leaving …

मैं … जा रहा /रही/ हूँ।
main … ja raha /rahī/ hūn.

We're leaving …

हम … जा रहे हैं।
ham … ja rahe hain.

right now

अभी
abhī

this afternoon

आज दोपहर
āj dopahar

tonight

आज रात
āj rāt

tomorrow

कल
kal

tomorrow morning

कल सुबह
kal subah

tomorrow evening

कल शाम
kal shām

the day after tomorrow

कल के बाद वाला दिन
kal ke bād vāla din

I'd like to pay.

मैं भुगतान करना चाहता /चाहती/ हूँ।
main bhugatān karana chāhata /chāhatī/ hūn.

Everything was wonderful.

सब कुछ बहुत अच्छा था।
sab kuchh bahut achchha tha.

Where can I get a taxi?

मुझे टैक्सी कहां मिलेगी?
mujhe taiksī kahān milegī?

Would you call a taxi for me, please?

क्या आप मेरे लिए एक टैक्सी बुला देंगे /देंगी/?
Kya āp mere lie ek taiksī bula denge /dengī/?

Restaurant

Can I look at the menu, please?
क्या आप अपना मेनू दिखा सकते हैं, प्लीज़?
kya āp apana menū dikha sakate hain, plīz?

Table for one.
एक के लिए टेबल।
ek ke lie tebal.

There are two (three, four) of us.
हम दो (तीन, चार) लोग हैं।
ham do (tīn, chār) log hain.

Smoking
स्मोकिंग
smoking

No smoking
नो स्मोकिंग
no smoking

Excuse me! (addressing a waiter)
एक्सक्यूज़ मी!
eksakyūz mī!

menu
मेनू
menū

wine list
वाइन सूची
vain sūchī

The menu, please.
मेनू ले आईये प्लीज़।
menū le āīye plīz.

Are you ready to order?
क्या आप ऑर्डर करने के लिए तैयार हैं?
kya āp ordar karane ke lie taiyār hain?

What will you have?
आप क्या लेना चाहेंगी /चाहेंगी/?
āp kya lena chāhengī /chāhengī/?

I'll have ...
मेरे लिए ... ले आईए।
mere lie ... le āīe.

I'm a vegetarian.
मैं शाकाहारी हूँ।
main shākāhārī hūn.

meat
माँस
māns

fish
मछली
machhalī

vegetables
सब्जियाँ
sabziyān

Do you have vegetarian dishes?
क्या आपके पास शाकाहारी पकवान है?
kya āpake pās shākāhārī pakavān hain?

I don't eat pork.
मैं सूअर का गोश्त नहीं खाता /खाती/ हूँ।
main sūar ka gosht nahin khāta /khātī/ hūn.

He /she/ doesn't eat meat.

वह माँस नहीं खाता /खाती/ है।
vah māns nahin khāta /khātī/ hai.

I am allergic to ...

मुझे ... से अलर्जी है।
mujhe ... se alarjī hai.

Would you please bring me ...

क्या आप मेरे लिए ... ले आएंगे प्लीज़
kya āp mere lie ... le āenge plīz

salt | pepper | sugar

नमक । काली मिर्च । चीनी
namak | kālī mirch | chīnī

coffee | tea | dessert

कॉफ़ी । चाय । मीठा
kofī | chāy | mītha

water | sparkling | plain

पानी । बुदबुदाने वाला पानी । सादा
pānī | budabudāne vāla pānī | sāda

a spoon | fork | knife

एक चम्मच । काँटा । चाकू
ek chammach | kānta | chākū

a plate | napkin

एक प्लेट । नैपकिन
ek plet | naipakin

Enjoy your meal!

अपने भोजन का आनंद लें!
apane bhojan ka ānand len!

One more, please.

एक और चाहिए।
ek aur chāhie.

It was very delicious.

वह अत्यंत स्वादिष्ट था।
vah atyant svādisht tha.

check | change | tip

चेक । छुट्टा । टिप
chek | chhutta | tip

Check, please.
(Could I have the check, please?)

चेक प्लीज़।
chek plīz.

Can I pay by credit card?

क्या मैं क्रेडिट कार्ड से पे कर
सकता /सकती/ हूँ
kya main kredit kārd se pe kar sakata
/sakatī/ hūn?

I'm sorry, there's a mistake here.

माफ़ कीजिएगा, यहाँ कुछ गलती है।
māf kījiega, yahān kuchh galatī hai.

Shopping

Can I help you?
क्या मैं आपकी मदद कर सकता /सकती/ हूँ?
kya main āpakī madad kar sakata /sakatī/ hūn?

Do you have ...?
क्या आपके पास ... है?
kya āpake pās ... hai?

I'm looking for ...
मैं ... ढूंढ रहा /रही/ हूँ।
main ... dhūnrh raha /rahī/ hūn.

I need ...
मुझे ... चाहिए।
mujhe ... chāhie.

I'm just looking.
मैं बस देख रहा /रही/ हूँ।
main bas dekh raha /rahī/ hūn.

We're just looking.
हम बस देख रहे हैं।
ham bas dekh rahe hain.

I'll come back later.
मैं बाद में वापिस आता /आती/ हूँ।
main bād men vāpis āta /ātī/ hūn.

We'll come back later.
हम बाद में वापिस आते हैं।
ham bād men vāpis āte hain.

discounts | sale
छूट | सेल
chhūt | sel

Would you please show me ...
क्या आप मुझे ... दिखाएंगे /दिखाएंगी/।
kya āp mujhe ... dikhaenge /dikhaengī/.

Would you please give me ...
क्या आप मुझे ... देंगे /देंगी/।
kya āp mujhe ... denge /dengī/.

Can I try it on?
क्या मैं इसे पहनकर देख सकता /सकती/ हूँ?
kya main isè pahanakar dekh sakata /sakatī/ hūn?

Excuse me, where's the fitting room?
माफ़ कीजिएगा, ट्राय रूम कहाँ है?
māf kījiega, trāy rūm kahān hai?

Which color would you like?
आपको कौन-सा रंग चाहिए?
āpako kaun-sa rang chāhie?

size | length
साइज़ | लंबाई
saiz | lambaī

How does it fit?
यह कैसा फिट होता है?
yah kaisa fit hota hai?

How much is it?
यह कितने का है?
yah kitane ka hai?

That's too expensive.
यह बहुत महंगा है।
yah bahut mahanga hai.

I'll take it.

मैं इसे ले लूँगा /लूँगी/।
main ise le lūnga /lūngī/.

Excuse me, where do I pay?

माफ़ कीजिएगा, पे कहाँ करना है?
māf kījiega, pe kahān karana hai?

Will you pay in cash or credit card?

क्या आप नकद में पे करेंगे या क्रेडिट कार्ड से?
kya āp nakad men pe karenge ya kredit kārd se?

In cash | with credit card

नकद में | क्रेडिट कार्ड से
nakad men | kredit kārd se

Do you want the receipt?

क्या आपको रसीद चाहिए?
kya āpako rasīd chāhie?

Yes, please.

हाँ, प्लीज़।
hān, plīz.

No, it's OK.

नहीं, ज़रूरत नहीं।
nahin, zarūrat nahin.

Thank you. Have a nice day!

शुक्रिया। आपका दिन शुभ हो।
shukriya. āpaka din shubh ho!

In town

Excuse me, please.	माफ़ कीजिएगा, ... māf kījiega, ...
I'm looking for ...	मैं ... ढूंढ रहा /रही/ हूँ। main ... dhūnrh raha /rahī/ hūn.
the subway	मेट्रो metro
my hotel	अपना होटल apana hotal
the movie theater	सिनेमा हॉल sinema hol
a taxi stand	टैक्सी स्टैंड taiksī staind

an ATM	एटीएम etīem
a foreign exchange office	मुद्रा विनिमय केंद्र foran eksachenj ofis
an internet café	साइबर कैफ़े saibar kaife
... street	... सड़क ... sarak
this place	यह जगह yah jagah

Do you know where ... is?	क्या आपको पता है कि ... कहाँ है? kya āpako pata hai ki ... kahān hai?
Which street is this?	यह कौन-सी सड़क है? yah kaun-sī sarak hai?
Show me where we are right now.	मुझे दिखाईये कि हम इस वक्त कहाँ है। mujhe dikhāīye ki ham is vakt kahān hain.
Can I get there on foot?	क्या मैं वहाँ पैदल जा सकता /सकती/ हूँ? kya main vahān paidal ja sakata /sakatī/ hūn?
Do you have a map of the city?	क्या आपके पास शहर का नक्शा है? kya āpake pās shahar ka naksha hai?

How much is a ticket to get in?	अंदर जाने का टिकट कितने का है? andar jāne ka tikat kitane ka hai?
Can I take pictures here?	क्या मैं यहाँ फोटो खींच सकता /सकती/ हूँ? kya main yāhan foto khīnch sakata /sakatī/ hūn?

Are you open? क्या यह जगह खुली है?
kya yah jagah khulī hai?

When do you open? आप इसे कब खोलते हैं?
āp ise kab kholate hain?

When do you close? आप इसे कब बंद करते हैं?
āp ise kab band karate hain?

Money

money	पैसा paisa
cash	नकद nakad
paper money	पेपर मनी pepar manī
loose change	सिक्के sikke
check | change | tip	चेक | छुट्टा | टिप chek | chhutta | tip
credit card	क्रेडिट कार्ड kredit kārd
wallet	बटुआ batua
to buy	खरीदना kharīdana
to pay	भुगतान करना bhugatān karana
fine	फाइन fain
free	मुफ्त muft
Where can I buy ...?	मैं ... कहाँ खरीद सकता /सकती/ हूँ? main ... kahā kharīd sakata /sakatī/ hūn?
Is the bank open now?	क्या बैंक इस वक्त खुला होगा? kya baink is vakt khula hoga?
When does it open?	वह कब खुलता है? vah kab khulata hai?
When does it close?	वह कब बंद होता है? vah kab band hota hai?
How much?	कितना? kitana?
How much is this?	यह कितने का है? yah kitane ka hai?
That's too expensive.	यह बहुत महंगा है yah bahut mahanga hai.
Excuse me, where do I pay?	माफ़ कीजिएगा, पे कहाँ करना है? māf kījiega, pe kahān karana hai?

Check, please.

चेक, प्लीज़।
chek, plīz.

Can I pay by credit card?

क्या मैं क्रेडिट कार्ड से पे कर
सकता /सकती/ हूँ?
kya main kredit kārd se pe kar
sakata /sakatī/ hūn?

Is there an ATM here?

क्या यहाँ पास में एटीएम है?
kya yahān pās men etīem hai?

I'm looking for an ATM.

मैं एटीएम ढूंढ रहा /रही/ हूँ।
main etīem dhūnrh raha /rahī/ hūn.

I'm looking for a foreign exchange office.

मैं मुद्रा विनिमय केंद्र ढूंढ रहा
/रही/ हूँ।
main mudra vinimay kendr dhūnrh raha
/rahī/ hūn.

I'd like to change …

मैं … बदलना चाहूँगा /चाहूँगी/।
main ... badalana chāhūngā /chāhūngī/.

What is the exchange rate?

एक्सचेंज रेट क्या है?
eksachenj ret kya hai?

Do you need my passport?

क्या मुझे पासपोर्ट की ज़रूरत है?
kya mujhe pāsaport kī zarūrat hai?

Time

What time is it?	क्या बजा है? kya baja hai?
When?	कब? kab?
At what time?	कितने बजे? kitane baje?
now | later | after ...	अभी | बाद में | ... के बाद abhī | bād men | ... ke bād
one o'clock	एक बजे ek baje
one fifteen	सवा एक बजे sava ek baje
one thirty	डेढ़ बजे derh baje
one forty-five	पौने दो बजे paune do baje
one | two | three	एक | दो | तीन ek | do | tīn
four | five | six	चार | पांच | छह chār | pānch | chhah
seven | eight | nine	सात | आठ | नौ sāt | āth | nau
ten | eleven | twelve	दस | ग्यारह | बारह das | gyārah | bārah
in ...	... में ... men
five minutes	पाँच मिनट pānch minat
ten minutes	दस मिनट das minat
fifteen minutes	पंद्रह मिनट pandrah minat
twenty minutes	बीस मिनट bīs minat
half an hour	आधे घंटे ādha ghanta
an hour	एक घंटे ek ghante
in the morning	सुबह में subah men
early in the morning	सुबह-सेवरे subah-sevare

this morning	इस सुबह
	is subah
tomorrow morning	कल सुबह
	kal subah

in the middle of the day	दोपहर में
	dopahar men
in the afternoon	दोपहर में
	dopahar men
in the evening	शाम में
	shām men
tonight	आज रात
	āj rāt

at night	रात को
	rāt ko
yesterday	कल
	kal
today	आज
	āj
tomorrow	कल
	kal
the day after tomorrow	कल के बाद वाला दिन
	kal ke bād vāla din

What day is it today?	आज कौन-सा दिन है?
	āj kaun-sa din hai?
It's ...	आज ... है।
	āj ... hai.
Monday	सोमवार
	somavār
Tuesday	मंगलवार
	mangalavār
Wednesday	बुधवार
	budhavār

Thursday	गुरुवार
	guruvār
Friday	शुक्रवार
	shukravār
Saturday	शनिवार
	shanivār
Sunday	रविवार
	ravivār

Greetings. Introductions

Hello.

नमस्कार
namaskār.

Pleased to meet you.

आपसे मिलकर ख़ुशी हुई
āpase milakar khushī huī.

Me too.

मुझे भी।
mujhe bhī.

I'd like you to meet ...

मैं आपको ... से मिलाना चाहूँगा
/चाहूँगी/।
main āpako ... se milāna chāhūnga
/chāhūngī/.

Nice to meet you.

आपसे मिलकर अच्छा लगा।
āpase milakar achchha laga.

How are you?

आप कैसे /कैसी/ हैं?
āp kaise /kaisī/ hain?

My name is ...

मेरा नाम ... है
mera nām ... hai.

His name is ...

इसका नाम ... है।
isaka nām ... hai.

Her name is ...

इसका नाम ... है।
isaka nām ... hai.

What's your name?

आपका क्या नाम है?
āpaka kya nām hai?

What's his name?

इसका क्या नाम है?
isaka kya nām hai?

What's her name?

इसका क्या नाम है?
isaka kya nām hai?

What's your last name?

आपका आख़िरी नाम क्या है?
āpaka ākhirī nām kya hai?

You can call me ...

आप मुझे ... बुला सकते /सकती/ हैं।
āp mujhe ... bula sakate /sakatī/ hain.

Where are you from?

आप कहाँ से हैं?
āp kahān se hain?

I'm from ...

मैं ... हूँ।
main ... hūn.

What do you do for a living?

आप क्या काम करते /करती/ हैं?
āp kya kām karate /karatī/ hain?

Who is this?

यह कौन है?
yah kaun hai?

Who is he?

यह कौन है?
yah kaun hai?

Who is she?	यह कौन है? yah kaun hai?
Who are they?	ये कौन हैं? ye kaun hain?

This is …	यह … है। yah … hai.
my friend (masc.)	मेरा दोस्त mera dost
my friend (fem.)	मेरी सहेली merī sahelī
my husband	मेरे पति mere pati
my wife	मेरी पत्नी merī patnī

my father	मेरे पिता mere pita
my mother	मेरी माँ merī mān
my brother	मेरे भाई mere bhaī
my sister	मेरी बहन merī bahan
my son	मेरा बेटा mera beta
my daughter	मेरी बेटी merī betī

This is our son.	यह मेरा बेटा है। yah mera betī hai.
This is our daughter.	यह मेरी बेटी है। yah merī betī hai.
These are my children.	ये मेरे बच्चे हैं। ye mere bachche hain.
These are our children.	ये हमारे बच्चे हैं। ye hamāre bachche hain.

Farewells

Good bye!	अलविदा! alavida!
Bye! (inform.)	बाय! bāy!
See you tomorrow.	कल मिलते हैं kal milate hain.
See you soon.	जल्दी मिलते हैं jaldī milate hain.
See you at seven.	सात बजे मिलते हैं sāt baje milate hain.
Have fun!	मज़े करो! maze karo!
Talk to you later.	बाद में बात करते हैं bād men bāt karate hain.
Have a nice weekend.	तुम्हारा सप्ताहांत शुभ रहे tumhāra saptāhānt shubh rahe.
Good night.	शुभ रात्रि shubh rātri.
It's time for me to go.	मेरे जाने का वक्त हो गया है mere jāne ka vakt ho gaya hai.
I have to go.	मुझे जाना होगा mujhe jāna hai.
I will be right back.	मैं अभी वापिस आता /आती/ हूँ main abhī vāpis āta /ātī/ hūn.
It's late.	देर हो गई है der ho gaī hai.
I have to get up early.	मुझे जल्दी उठना है mujhe jaldī uthana hai.
I'm leaving tomorrow.	मैं कल जाने वाला /वाली/ हूँ main kal jāne vāla /vālī/ hūn.
We're leaving tomorrow.	हम कल जाने वाले हैं ham kal jāne vāle hain.
Have a nice trip!	आपकी यात्रा शानदार हो! āpakī yātra shānadār ho!
It was nice meeting you.	आपसे मिलकर अच्छा लगा āpase milakar achchha laga.
It was nice talking to you.	आपसे बातें करके अच्छा लगा āpase bāten karake achchha laga.
Thanks for everything.	हर चीज़ के लिए शुक्रिया har chīz ke lie shukriya.

I had a very good time.

मैंने बहुत अच्छा वक्त बिताया।
mainne bahut achchha vakt bitāya.

We had a very good time.

हमने बहुत बहुत अच्छा वक्त बिताया।
hamane bahut achchha vakt bitāya.

It was really great.

बहुत मज़ा आया।
bahut maza āya.

I'm going to miss you.

मुझे तुम्हारी याद आएगी।
mujhe tumhārī yād āegī.

We're going to miss you.

हमें आपकी याद आएगी।
hamen āpakī yād āegī.

Good luck!

गुड लक!
gud lak!

Say hi to ...

... को नमस्ते बोलना।
... ko namaste bolana.

Foreign language

I don't understand.	मुझे समझ नहीं आया। mujhe samajh nahin āya.
Write it down, please.	इसे लिख दीजिए, प्लीज़। ise likh dījie, plīz.
Do you speak …?	क्या आप … बोलते /बोलती/ हैं? kya āp … bolate /bolatī/ hain?

I speak a little bit of …	मैं थोड़ा-बहुत … बोल सकता /सकती/ हूँ। main thora-bahut … bol sakata /sakatī/ hūn.
English	अंग्रेज़ी angrezī

Turkish	तुर्की turkī
Arabic	अरबी arabī
French	फ्रांसिसी frānsisī

German	जर्मन jarman
Italian	इतालवी itālavī
Spanish	स्पेनी spenī

Portuguese	पुर्तगाली purtagālī
Chinese	चीनी chīnī
Japanese	जापानी jāpānī

Can you repeat that, please.	क्या आप इसे दोहरा सकते हैं। kya āp ise dohara sakate hain.
I understand.	मैं समझ गया /गई/। main samajh gaya /gaī/.
I don't understand.	मुझे समझ नहीं आया। mujhe samajh nahin āya.
Please speak more slowly.	कृपया थोड़ा और धीरे बोलिये। krpaya thora aur dhīre boliye.

Is that correct? (Am I saying it right?)

क्या यह सही है?
kya yah sahī hai?

What is this? (What does this mean?)

यह क्या है?
yah kya hai?

Apologies

Excuse me, please.

मुझे माफ़ करना।
mujhe māf karana.

I'm sorry.

मुझे माफ़ कर दो।
mujhe māf karana.

I'm really sorry.

मैं बहुत शर्मिन्दा हूँ।
main bahut sharminda hūn.

Sorry, it's my fault.

माफ़ करना, यह मेरी गलती है।
māf karana, yah merī galatī hai.

My mistake.

मेरी गलती।
merī galatī.

May I ...?

क्या मैं ... सकता /सकती/ हूँ?
kya main ... sakata /sakatī/ hūn?

Do you mind if I ...?

क्या मैं ... सकता /सकती/ हूँ?
kya main ... sakata /sakatī/ hūn?

It's OK.

कोई बात नहीं।
koī bāt nahin.

It's all right.

सब कुछ ठीक है।
sab kuchh thīk hai.

Don't worry about it.

फिक्र मत करो।
fikr mat karo.

Agreement

Yes.
हाँ।
hān.

Yes, sure.
हाँ, बिल्कुल।
hān, bilkul.

OK (Good!)
ओके! बढ़िया!
oke! barhiya!

Very well.
ठीक है।
thīk hai.

Certainly!
बिल्कुल!
bilkul!

I agree.
मैं सहमत हूँ।
main sahamat hūn.

That's correct.
यह सही है।
yah sahī hai.

That's right.
यह ठीक है।
yah thīk hai.

You're right.
आप सही हैं।
āp sahī hain.

I don't mind.
मुझे बुरा नहीं लगेगा।
mujhe bura nahin lagega.

Absolutely right.
बिल्कुल सही।
bilkul sahī.

It's possible.
हो सकता है।
ho sakata hai.

That's a good idea.
यह अच्छा विचार है।
yah achchha vichār hai.

I can't say no.
मैं नहीं नहीं बोल सकता
/सकती/ हूँ।
main nahin nahin bol sakata
/sakatī/ hūn.

I'd be happy to.
मुझे ख़ुश होगी।
mujhe khush hogī.

With pleasure.
ख़ुशी से।
khushī se.

Refusal. Expressing doubt

No.	नहीं। nahin.
Certainly not.	बिल्कुल नहीं। bilkul nahin.
I don't agree.	मैं सहमत नहीं हूँ। main sahamat nahin hūn.
I don't think so.	मुझे नहीं लगता है। mujhe nahin lagata hai.
It's not true.	यह सही नहीं है। yah sahī nahin hai.
You are wrong.	आप गलत हैं। āp galat hain.
I think you are wrong.	मेरे ख्याल में आप गलत हैं। mere khyāl men āp galat hain.
I'm not sure.	मुझे पक्का नहीं पता है। mujhe pakka nahin pata hai.
It's impossible.	यह मुमकिन नहीं है। yah mumakin nahin hai.
Nothing of the kind (sort)!	ऐसा कुछ नहीं हुआ! aisa kuchh nahin hua!
The exact opposite.	इससे बिल्कुल उलटा। isase bilkul ulata.
I'm against it.	मैं इसके खिलाफ़ हूँ। main isake khilāf hūn.
I don't care.	मुझे कोई फर्क नहीं पड़ता। mujhe koī fark nahin parata.
I have no idea.	मुझे कुछ नहीं पता। mujhe kuchh nahin pata.
I doubt it.	मुझे इस बात पर शक है। mujhe is bāt par shak hai.
Sorry, I can't.	माफ़ करना, मैं नहीं कर सकता /सकती/ हूँ। māf karana, main nahin kar sakata /sakatī/ hūn.
Sorry, I don't want to.	माफ़ करना, मैं नहीं करना चाहता /चाहती/ हूँ। māf karana, main nahin karana chāhata /chāhatī/ hūn.
Thank you, but I don't need this.	शुक्रिया, मगर मुझे इसकी ज़रूरत नहीं है। shukriya, magar mujhe isakī zarūrat nahin hai.

It's getting late.

देर हो रही है।
der ho rahī hai.

I have to get up early.

मुझे जल्दी उठना है।
mujhe jaldī uthana hai.

I don't feel well.

मेरी तबियत ठीक नहीं है।
merī tabiyat thīk nahin hai.

Expressing gratitude

Thank you.
शुक्रिया।
shukriya.

Thank you very much.
बहुत बहुत शुक्रिया।
bahut bahut shukriya.

I really appreciate it.
मैं बहुत आभारी हूँ।
main bahut ābhārī hūn.

I'm really grateful to you.
मैं बहुत बहुत आभारी हूँ।
main bahut bahut ābhārī hūn.

We are really grateful to you.
हम बहुत आभारी हैं।
ham bahut ābhārī hain.

Thank you for your time.
आपके वक्त के लिए शुक्रिया।
āpake vakt ke lie shukriya.

Thanks for everything.
हर चीज़ के लिए शुक्रिया।
har chīz ke lie shukriya.

Thank you for ...
... के लिए शुक्रिया।
... ke lie shukriya.

your help
आपकी मदद
āpakī madad

a nice time
अच्छे वक्त
achchhe vakt

a wonderful meal
बढ़िया खाने
barhiya khāne

a pleasant evening
खुशनुमा शाम
khushanuma shām

a wonderful day
बढ़िया दिन
barhiya din

an amazing journey
अद्भुत सफर
adbhut safar

Don't mention it.
शुक्रिया की कोई ज़रूरत नहीं।
shukriya kī koī zarūrat nahin.

You are welcome.
आपका स्वागत है।
āpaka svāgat hai.

Any time.
कभी भी।
kabhī bhī.

My pleasure.
यह मेरे लिए खुशी की बात है।
yah mere lie khushī kī bāt hai.

Forget it.
भूल जाओ।
bhūl jao.

Don't worry about it.
फिक्र मत करो।
fikr mat karo.

Congratulations. Best wishes

Congratulations!
मुबारक हो!
mubārak ho!

Happy birthday!
जन्मदिन की बधाई!
janmadin kī badhaī!

Merry Christmas!
बड़ा दिन मुबारक हो!
bara din mubārak ho!

Happy New Year!
नए साल की बधाई!
nae sāl kī badhaī!

Happy Easter!
ईस्टर की शुभकामनाएं!
īstar kī shubhakāmanaen!

Happy Hanukkah!
हनुका की बधाईयाँ!
hanuka kī badhaīyān!

I'd like to propose a toast.
मैं एक टोस्ट करना चाहूँगा
/चाहूँगी/।
main ek tost karana chāhūnga
/chāhūngī/.

Cheers!
चियर्स!
chiyars!

Let's drink to …!
… के लिए पीया जाए!
… ke lie pīya jae!

To our success!
हमारी कामियाबी!
hamārī kāmiyābī!

To your success!
आपकी कामियाबी!
āpakī kāmiyābī!

Good luck!
गुड लक!
gud lak!

Have a nice day!
आपका दिन शुभ हो!
āpaka din shubh ho!

Have a good holiday!
आपकी छुट्टी अच्छी रहे!
āpakī chhuttī achchhī rahe!

Have a safe journey!
आपका सफर सुरक्षित रहे!
āpaka safar surakshit rahe!

I hope you get better soon!
मैं उम्मीद करता /करती/ हूँ कि
आप जल्द ही ठीक हो जाएंगे!
main ummīd karata /karatī/ hūn
ki āp jald hī thīk ho jaenge!

Socializing

Why are you sad?	आप उदास क्यों हैं? āp udās kyon hain?
Smile! Cheer up!	मुस्कुराओ! खुश रहो! muskurao! khush raho!
Are you free tonight?	क्या आप आज रात फ्री हैं? kya āp āj rāt frī hain?
May I offer you a drink?	क्या मैं आपके लिए एक ड्रिंक खरीद सकता /सकती/ हूँ? kya main āpake lie ek drink kharīd sakata /sakatī/ hūn?
Would you like to dance?	क्या आप डांस करना चाहेंगी /चाहेंगी/? kya āp dāns karana chāhengī /chāhengī/?
Let's go to the movies.	चलिए फ़िल्म देखने चलते हैं। chalie film dekhane chalate hain.
May I invite you to …?	क्या मैं आपको … इन्वाइट कर सकता /सकती/ हूँ? kya main āpako … invait kar sakata /sakatī/ hūn?
a restaurant	रेस्तरां restarān
the movies	फ़िल्म के लिए film ke lie
the theater	थियेटर के लिए thiyetar ke lie
go for a walk	वॉक के लिए vok ke lie
At what time?	कितने बजे? kitane baje?
tonight	आज रात āj rāt
at six	छह बजे chhah baje
at seven	सात बजे sāt baje
at eight	आठ बजे āth baje
at nine	नौ बजे nau baje

Do you like it here?	क्या आपको यहाँ अच्छा लगता है? kya āpako yahān achchha lagata hai?
Are you here with someone?	क्या आप यहाँ किसी के साथ आए /आई/ हैं? kya āp yahān kisī ke sāth āe /āī/ hain?
I'm with my friend.	मैं अपने दोस्त के साथ हूँ। main apane dost ke sāth hūn.
I'm with my friends.	मैं अपने दोस्तों के साथ हूँ। main apane doston ke sāth hūn.
No, I'm alone.	नहीं, मैं अकेला /अकेली/ हूँ। nahin, main akela /akelī/ hūn.
Do you have a boyfriend?	क्या आपका कोई बॉयफ्रेंड है? kya āpaka koī boyafrend hai?
I have a boyfriend.	मेरा बॉयफ्रेंड है। mera boyafrend hai.
Do you have a girlfriend?	क्या आपकी कोई गर्लफ्रेंड है? kya āpakī koī garlafrend hai?
I have a girlfriend.	मेरी एक गर्लफ्रेंड है। merī ek garlafrend hai.
Can I see you again?	क्या आपसे फिर मिल सकता /सकती/ हूँ? kya āpase fir mil sakata /sakatī/ hūn?
Can I call you?	क्या मैं आपको कॉल कर सकता /सकती/ हूँ? kya main āpako kol kar sakata /sakatī/ hūn?
Call me. (Give me a call.)	मुझे कॉल करना। mujhe kol karana.
What's your number?	आपका नंबर क्या है? āpaka nambar kya hai?
I miss you.	मुझे तुम्हारी याद आ रही है। mujhe tumhārī yād ā rahī hai.
You have a beautiful name.	आपका नाम बहुत खूबसूरत है। āpaka nām bahut khūbasūrat hai.
I love you.	मैं तुमसे प्यार करता /करती/ हूँ। main tumase pyār karata /karatī/ hūn.
Will you marry me?	क्या तुम मुझसे शादी करोगे /करोगी/? kya tum mujhase shādī karoge /karogī/?
You're kidding!	तुम मज़ाक कर रहे /रही/ हो! tum mazāk kar rahe /rahī/ ho!
I'm just kidding.	मैं बस मज़ाक कर रहा रही हूँ। main bas mazāk kar raha rahī hūn.
Are you serious?	क्या आप सीरियस हैं? kya āp sīriyas hain?
I'm serious.	मैं सीरियस हूँ। main sīriyas hūn.

Really?!

सच में?!
sach men?!

It's unbelievable!

मुझे यकिन नहीं होता!
mujhe yakin nahin hota!

I don't believe you.

मुझे तुम पर यकिन नहीं है।
mujhe tum par yakin nahin hai.

I can't.

मैं नहीं आ सकता /सकती/।
main nahin ā sakata /sakatī/.

I don't know.

मुझे नहीं मालूम।
mujhe nahin mālūm.

I don't understand you.

मुझे आपकी बात समझ नहीं आई।
mujhe āpakī bāt samajh nahin āī.

Please go away.

यहाँ से चले जाईये।
yahān se chale jaīye.

Leave me alone!

मुझे अकेला छोड़ दो!
mujhe akela chhor do!

I can't stand him.

मैं उसे बर्दाश्त नहीं कर सकता
/सकती/ हूँ।
main use bārdāsht nahin kar sakata
/sakatī/ hūn.

You are disgusting!

तुमसे घिन्न आती है!
tumase ghinn ātī hai!

I'll call the police!

मैं पुलिस बुला लूँगा /लूँगी/!
main pulis bula lūnga /lūngī/!

Sharing impressions. Emotions

I like it.
मुझे यह पसंद है।
mujhe yah pasand hai.

Very nice.
बहुत अच्छा।
bahut achchha.

That's great!
बहुत बढ़िया!
bahut barhiya!

It's not bad.
बुरा नहीं है।
bura nahin hai.

I don't like it.
मुझे यह पसंद नहीं है।
mujhe yah pasand nahin hai.

It's not good.
यह अच्छा नहीं है।
yah achchha nahin hai.

It's bad.
यह बुरा है।
yah bura hai.

It's very bad.
यह बहुत बुरा है।
yah bahut bura hai.

It's disgusting.
यह घिनौना है।
yah ghinauna hai.

I'm happy.
मैं खुश हूँ।
main khush hūn.

I'm content.
मैं संतुष्ट हूँ।
main santusht hūn.

I'm in love.
मुझे प्यार हो गया है।
mujhe pyār ho gaya hai.

I'm calm.
मैं शांत हूँ।
main shānt hūn.

I'm bored.
मुझे बोरियत हो रही है।
mujhe boriyat ho rahī hai.

I'm tired.
मैं थक गया /गई/ हूँ।
main thak gaya /gaī/ hūn.

I'm sad.
मैं दुखी हूँ।
main dukhī hūn.

I'm frightened.
मुझे डर लग रहा हैं।
mujhe dar lag raha hain.

I'm angry.
मुझे गुस्सा आ रहा है।
mujhe gussa ā raha hai.

I'm worried.
मैं परेशान हूँ।
main pareshān hūn.

I'm nervous.
मुझे घवराहट हो रही है।
mujhe ghavarāhat ho rahī hai.

I'm jealous. (envious)

मुझे जलन हो रही है।
mujhe jalan ho rahī hai.

I'm surprised.

मुझे हैरानी हो रही है।
mujhe hairānī ho rahī hai.

I'm perplexed.

मुझे समझ नहीं आ रहा है।
mujhe samajh nahin ā raha hai.

Problems. Accidents

I've got a problem.
मुझे एक परेशानी है।
mujhe ek pareshānī hai.

We've got a problem.
हमें परेशानी है।
hamen pareshānī hai.

I'm lost.
मैं खो गया /गई/ हूँ।
main kho gaya /gaī/ hūn.

I missed the last bus (train).
मुझसे आखिरी बस छूट गई।
mujhase ākhirī bas chhūt gaī.

I don't have any money left.
मेरे पास पैसे नहीं बचे।
mere pās paise nahin bache.

I've lost my …
मेरा … खो गया है।
mera … kho gaya hai.

Someone stole my …
किसी ने मेरा … चुरा लिया।
kisī ne mera … churā liya.

passport
पासपोर्ट
pāsaport

wallet
बटुआ
batua

papers
कागज़ात
kāgazāt

ticket
टिकट
tikat

money
पैसा
paisa

handbag
पर्स
pars

camera
कैमरा
kaimara

laptop
लैपटॉप
laipatop

tablet computer
टैबलेट
taibalet

mobile phone
मोबाइल फ़ोन
mobail fon

Help me!
मेरी मदद करो!
merī madad karo!

What's happened?
क्या हुआ?
kya hua?

fire
आग
āg

shooting
गोलियाँ चल रही हैं
goliyān chal rahī hain

murder	कत्ल हो गया है
	katl ho gaya hai
explosion	विस्फोट हो गया है
	visfot ho gaya hai
fight	लड़ाई हो गई है
	laraī ho gaī hai

Call the police!	पुलिस को बुलाओ!
	pulis ko bulāo!
Please hurry up!	कृपया जल्दी करें!
	kṛpaya jaldī karen!
I'm looking for the police station.	मैं पुलिस थाना ढूँढ रहा /रही/ हूँ।
	main pulis thāna dhūnrh raha /rahī/ hūn.
I need to make a call.	मुझे फ़ोन करना है।
	mujhe fon karana hai.
May I use your phone?	क्या मैं आपका फ़ोन इस्तेमाल कर सकता /सकती/ हूँ?
	kya main āpaka fon istemāl kar sakata /sakatī/ hūn?

mugged	मेरा सामान चुरा लिया गया है
	mera sāmān chura liya gaya hai
robbed	मुझे लूट लिया गया है
	mujhe lūt liya gaya hai
raped	मेरा बालात्कार किया गया है
	mera bālātkār kiya gaya hai
attacked (beaten up)	मुझे पीटा गया है
	mujhe pīta gaya hai

Are you all right?	क्या आप ठीक हैं?
	kya āp thīk hain?
Did you see who it was?	क्या आपने देखा कौन था?
	kya āpane dekha kaun tha?
Would you be able to recognize the person?	क्या आप उसे पहचान सकेंगे /सकेंगी/?
	kya āp use pahachān sakenge /sakengī/?
Are you sure?	क्या आपको यकीन है?
	kya āpako yakīn hai?

Please calm down.	कृपया शांत हो जाएं।
	kṛpaya shānt ho jaen.
Take it easy!	आराम से!
	ārām se!
Don't worry!	चिंता मत करो!
	chinta mat karo!
Everything will be fine.	सब ठीक हो जायेगा।
	sab thīk ho jāyega.
Everything's all right.	सब कुछ ठीक है।
	sab kuchh thīk hai.
Come here, please.	कृपया यहाँ आइये।
	kṛpaya yahān āiye.

I have some questions for you.

मेरे पास तुम्हारे लिए कुछ प्रश्न है।
mere pās tumhāre lie kuchh prashn hai.

Wait a moment, please.

कृपया एक क्षण रुकें।
kṛpaya ek kshan ruken.

Do you have any I.D.?

क्या आपके पास आईडी है?
kya āpake pās āīdī hai?

Thanks. You can leave now.

धन्यवाद। आप अब जा सकते
/सकती/ हैं।
dhanyavād. āp ab ja sakate
/sakatī/ hain.

Hands behind your head!

अपने हाथ सिर के पीछे रखें!
apane hāth sir ke pīchhe rakhen!

You're under arrest!

आप हिरासत में हैं!
āp hirāsat men hain!

Health problems

Please help me.	कृपया मेरी मदद करें। kŕpaya merī madad karen.
I don't feel well.	मेरी तबियत ठीक नहीं है। merī tabiyat thīk nahin hai.
My husband doesn't feel well.	मेरे पति को ठीक महसूस नहीं हो रहा है। mere pati ko thīk mahasūs nahin ho raha hai.
My son ...	मेरे बेटे ... mere bete ...
My father ...	मेरे पिता ... mere pita ...
My wife doesn't feel well.	मेरी पत्नी को ठीक महसूस नहीं हो रहा है। merī patnī ko thīk mahasūs nahin ho raha hai.
My daughter ...	मेरी बेटी ... merī betī ...
My mother ...	मेरी माँ ... merī mān ...
headache	मुझे सिरदर्द है। mujhe siradard hai.
sore throat	मेरा गला ख़राब है। mera gala kharāb hai.
stomach ache	मेरे पेट में दर्द है। mere pet men dard hai.
toothache	मेरे दाँत में दर्द है। mere dānt men dard hai.
I feel dizzy.	मुझे चक्कर आ रहा है। mujhe chakkar ā raha hai.
He has a fever.	इसे बुखार है। ise bukhār hai.
She has a fever.	इसे बुखार है। ise bukhār hai.
I can't breathe.	मैं साँस नहीं ले पा रहा /रही/ हूँ। main sāns nahin le pa raha /rahī/ hūn.
I'm short of breath.	मेरी साँस फूल रही है। merī sāns fūl rahī hai.
I am asthmatic.	मुझे दमा है। mujhe dama hai.

I am diabetic.

मैं मधुमेह का /की/ रोगी हूँ।
main madhumeh ka /kī/ rogī hūn.

I can't sleep.

मैं सो नहीं पा रहा /रही/ हूँ।
main so nahin pa raha /rahī/ hūn.

food poisoning

फ़ुड पॉएज़निंग
fūd poezaning

It hurts here.

यहाँ दुखता हैं।
yahān dukhata hain.

Help me!

मेरी मदद करो!
merī madad karo!

I am here!

मैं यहाँ हूँ!
main yahān hūn!

We are here!

हम यहाँ हैं!
ham yahān hain!

Get me out of here!

मुझे यहां से बाहर निकालो!
mujhe yahān se bāhar nikālo!

I need a doctor.

मुझे एक डॉक्टर की ज़रुरत है।
mujhe ek doktar kī zarurat hai.

I can't move.

मैं हिल नहीं सकता /सकती/ हूँ।
main hil nahin sakata /sakatī/ hūn.

I can't move my legs.

मैं अपने पैरों को नहीं हिला
पा रहा /रही/ हूँ।
main apane pairon ko nahin hila
pa raha /rahī/ hūn.

I have a wound.

मुझे चोट लगी है।
mujhe chot lagī hai.

Is it serious?

क्या यह गंभीर है?
kya yah gambhīr hai?

My documents are in my pocket.

मेरे दस्तावेज़ मेरी जेब में हैं।
mere dastāvez merī jeb men hain.

Calm down!

शांत हो जाओ!
shānt ho jao!

May I use your phone?

क्या मैं आपका फ़ोन इस्तेमाल
कर सकता /सकती/ हूँ?
kya main āpaka fon istemāl
kar sakata /sakatī/ hūn?

Call an ambulance!

एम्बुलेन्स बुलाओ!
embulens bulao!

It's urgent!

बहुत ज़रूरी है!
bahut zarūrī hai!

It's an emergency!

यह एक आपातकाल है!
yah ek āpātakāl hai!

Please hurry up!

कृपया जल्दी करें!
krpaya jaldī karen!

Would you please call a doctor?

क्या आप डॉक्टर को बुला देंगे /देंगी/?
kya āp doktar ko bula denge /dengī/?

Where is the hospital?

अस्पताल कहाँ है?
aspatāl kahān hai?

How are you feeling?

आप कैसा महसूस कर रहे /रही/ हैं?
āp kaisa mahasūs kar rahe /rahī/ hain?

Are you all right?

क्या आप ठीक हैं?
kya āp thīk hain?

What's happened?

क्या हुआ?
kya hūa?

I feel better now.

मैं अब ठीक हूँ।
main ab thīk hūn.

It's OK.

सब ठीक है।
sab thīk hai.

It's all right.

सब कुछ ठीक है।
sab kuchh thīk hai.

At the pharmacy

pharmacy (drugstore)

दवा की दुकान
dava kī dukān

24-hour pharmacy

चौबीस घंटे खुलने वाली
दवा की दुकान
chaubīs ghante khulane vālī
dava kī dukān

Where is the closest pharmacy?

सबसे करीबी दवा की दुकान कहाँ है?
sabase karībī dava kī dukān kahān hai?

Is it open now?

क्या वह अभी खुली है?
kya vah abhī khulī hai?

At what time does it open?

वह कितने बजे खुलती है?
vah kitane baje khulatī hai?

At what time does it close?

वह कितने बजे बंद होती है?
vah kitane baje band hotī hai?

Is it far?

क्या वह दूर है?
kya vah dūr hai?

Can I get there on foot?

क्या मैं वहाँ पैदल जा सकता
/सकती/ हूँ?
kya main vahān paidal ja sakata
/sakatī/ hūn?

Can you show me on the map?

क्या आप मुझे नक्शे पर दिखा
सकते /सकती/ हैं?
kya āp mujhe nakshe par dikha
sakate /sakatī/ hain?

Please give me something for …

मुझे … के लिए कुछ दे दें।
mujhe … ke lie kuchh de den.

a headache

सिरदर्द
siradard

a cough

खाँसी
khānsī

a cold

ज़ुकाम
zukām

the flu

ज़ुकाम-बुखार
zukām-bukhār

a fever

बुखार
bukhār

a stomach ache

पेट दर्द
pet dard

nausea

मतली
matalī

diarrhea	दस्त
	dast
constipation	कब्ज़
	kabz

pain in the back	पीठ दर्द
	pīth dard
chest pain	सीने में दर्द
	sīne men dard
side stitch	पेट की माँसपेशी में दर्द
	pet kī mānsapeshī men dard
abdominal pain	पेट दर्द
	pet dard

pill	दवा
	dava
ointment, cream	मरहम, क्रीम
	maraham, krīm
syrup	सिरप
	sirap
spray	स्प्रे
	spre
drops	ड्रॉप
	drop

You need to go to the hospital.	आपको अस्पताल जाना चाहिए।
	āpako aspatāl jāna chāhie.
health insurance	स्वास्थ्य बीमा
	svāsthy bīma
prescription	नुस्खा
	nuskha
insect repellant	कीटरोधक
	kītarodhak
Band Aid	बैंड एड
	baind ed

The bare minimum

Excuse me, ...	माफ़ कीजिएगा, ... māf kījiega, ...
Hello.	नमस्कार। namaskār.
Thank you.	शुक्रिया। shukriya.
Good bye.	अलविदा। alavida.
Yes.	हाँ। hān.
No.	नहीं। nahin.
I don't know.	मुझे नहीं मालूम। mujhe nahin mālūm.
Where? | Where to? | When?	कहाँ? | कहाँ जाना है? | कब? kahān? | kahān jāna hai? | kab?
I need ...	मुझे ... चाहिए। mujhe ... chāhie.
I want ...	मैं ... चाहता /चाहती/ हूँ। main ... chāhata /chāhatī/ hūn.
Do you have ...?	क्या आपके पास ... है? kya āpake pās ... hai?
Is there a ... here?	क्या यहाँ ... है? kya yahān ... hai?
May I ...?	क्या मैं ... सकता /सकती/ हूँ? kya main ... sakata /sakatī/ hūn?
..., please (polite request)	..., कृपया। ..., krpaya.
I'm looking for ...	मैं ... ढूंढ रहा /रही/ हूँ। main ... dhūnrh raha /rahī/ hūn.
restroom	शौचालय shauchālay
ATM	एटीएम etīem
pharmacy (drugstore)	दवा की दुकान dava kī dūkān
hospital	अस्पताल aspatāl
police station	पुलिस थाना pulis thāna
subway	मेट्रो metro

taxi	टैक्सी taiksī
train station	ट्रेन स्टेशन tren steshan

My name is ...	मेरा नाम ... है। mera nām ... hai
What's your name?	आपका क्या नाम है? āpaka kya nām hai?
Could you please help me?	क्या आप मेरी मदद कर सकते /सकती/ हैं? kya āp merī madad kar sakate /sakatī/ hain?
I've got a problem.	मुझे एक परेशानी है। mujhe ek pareshānī hai.
I don't feel well.	मेरी तबियत ठीक नहीं है। merī tabiyat thīk nahin hai.
Call an ambulance!	एम्बुलेन्स बुलाओ! embulens bulao!
May I make a call?	क्या मैं एक फ़ोन कर सकता /सकती/ हूँ? kya main ek fon kar sakata /sakatī/ hūn?

I'm sorry.	मुझे माफ़ करना। mujhe māf kar do.
You're welcome.	आपका स्वागत है। āpaka svāgat hai.

I, me	मैं main
you (inform.)	तू tū
he	वह vah
she	वह vah
they (masc.)	वे ve
they (fem.)	वे ve
we	हम ham
you (pl)	तुम tum
you (sg, form.)	आप āp

ENTRANCE	प्रवेश pravesh
EXIT	निकास nikās

OUT OF ORDER

ख़राब है
kharāb hai

CLOSED

बंद
band

OPEN

खुला
khula

FOR WOMEN

महिलाओं के लिए
mahilaon ke lie

FOR MEN

पुरूषों के लिए
purūshon ke lie

T&P BOOKS

TOPICAL
VOCABULARY

This section contains more than 3,000 of the most important words.
The dictionary will provide invaluable assistance while traveling abroad, because frequently individual words are enough for you to be understood.
The dictionary includes a convenient transcription of each foreign word

T&P Books Publishing

VOCABULARY
CONTENTS

T&P Books Publishing

T&P BOOKS

BASIC CONCEPTS

T&P Books Publishing

1. Pronouns

I, me	मैं	main
you	तुम	tum
he, she, it	वह	vah
we	हम	ham
you (to a group)	आप	āp
they	वे	ve

2. Greetings. Salutations

Hello! (fam.)	नमस्कार!	namaskār!
Hello! (form.)	नमस्ते!	namaste!
Good morning!	नमस्ते!	namaste!
Good afternoon!	नमस्ते!	namaste!
Good evening!	नमस्ते!	namaste!
to say hello	नमस्कार कहना	namaskār kahana
Hi! (hello)	नमस्कार!	namaskār!
greeting (n)	अभिवादन (m)	abhivādan
to greet (vt)	अभिवादन करना	abhivādan karana
How are you?	आप कैसे हैं?	āp kaise hain?
What's new?	क्या हाल है?	kya hāl hai?
Bye-Bye! Goodbye!	अलविदा!	alavida!
See you soon!	फिर मिलेंगे!	fir milenge!
Farewell! (to a friend)	अलिवदा!	alivada!
Farewell! (form.)	अलविदा!	alavida!
to say goodbye	अलविदा कहना	alavida kahana
So long!	अलविदा!	alavida!
Thank you!	धन्यवाद!	dhanyavād!
Thank you very much!	बहुत बहुत शुक्रिया!	bahut bahut shukriya!
You're welcome	कोई बात नहीं	koī bāt nahin
Don't mention it!	कोई बात नहीं	koī bāt nahin
It was nothing	कोई बात नहीं	koī bāt nahin
Excuse me! (fam.)	माफ़ कीजिएगा!	māf kījiega!
Excuse me! (form.)	माफ़ी कीजियेगा!	māfī kījiyega!
to excuse (forgive)	माफ़ करना	māf karana
to apologize (vi)	माफ़ी मांगना	māfī māngana
My apologies	मुझे माफ़ कीजिएगा	mujhe māf kījiega

I'm sorry!	मुझे माफ़ कीजिएगा!	mujhe māf kījiega!
to forgive (vt)	माफ़ करना	māf karana
please (adv)	कृप्या	krpya

Don't forget!	भूलना नहीं!	bhūlana nahin!
Certainly!	ज़रूर!	zarūr!
Of course not!	बिल्कुल नहीं!	bilkul nahin!
Okay! (I agree)	ठीक है!	thīk hai!
That's enough!	बहुत हुआ!	bahut hua!

3. Questions

Who?	कौन?	kaun?
What?	क्या?	kya?
Where? (at, in)	कहाँ?	kahān?
Where (to)?	किधर?	kidhar?
From where?	कहाँ से?	kahān se?
When?	कब?	kab?
Why? (What for?)	क्यों?	kyon?
Why? (~ are you crying?)	क्यों?	kyon?

What for?	किस लिये?	kis liye?
How? (in what way)	कैसे?	kaise?
What? (What kind of ...?)	कौन-सा?	kaun-sa?
Which?	कौन-सा?	kaun-sa?

To whom?	किसको?	kisako?
About whom?	किसके बारे में?	kisake bāre men?
About what?	किसके बारे में?	kisake bāre men?
With whom?	किसके?	kisake?

How many? How much?	कितना?	kitana?
Whose?	किसका?	kisaka?

4. Prepositions

with (accompanied by)	के साथ	ke sāth
without	के बिना	ke bina
to (indicating direction)	की तरफ़	kī taraf
about (talking ~ ...)	के बारे में	ke bāre men
before (in time)	के पहले	ke pahale
in front of ...	के सामने	ke sāmane

under (beneath, below)	के नीचे	ke nīche
above (over)	के ऊपर	ke ūpar
on (atop)	पर	par
from (off, out of)	से	se
of (made from)	से	se

in (e.g., ~ ten minutes)	में	men
over (across the top of)	के ऊपर चढ़कर	ke ūpar charhakar

5. Function words. Adverbs. Part 1

Where? (at, in)	कहाँ?	kahān?
here (adv)	यहाँ	yahān
there (adv)	वहां	vahān
somewhere (to be)	कहीं	kahīn
nowhere (not anywhere)	कहीं नहीं	kahīn nahin
by (near, beside)	के पास	ke pās
by the window	खिड़की के पास	khirakī ke pās
Where (to)?	किधर?	kidhar?
here (e.g., come ~!)	इधर	idhar
there (e.g., to go ~)	उधर	udhar
from here (adv)	यहां से	yahān se
from there (adv)	वहां से	vahān se
close (adv)	पास	pās
far (adv)	दूर	dūr
near (e.g., ~ Paris)	निकट	nikat
nearby (adv)	पास	pās
not far (adv)	दूर नहीं	dūr nahin
left (adj)	बायाँ	bāyān
on the left	बायीं तरफ़	bāyīn taraf
to the left	बायीं तरफ़	bāyīn taraf
right (adj)	दायां	dāyān
on the right	दायीं तरफ़	dāyīn taraf
to the right	दायीं तरफ़	dāyīn taraf
in front (adv)	सामने	sāmane
front (as adj)	सामने का	sāmane ka
ahead (the kids ran ~)	आगे	āge
behind (adv)	पीछे	pīchhe
from behind	पीछे से	pīchhe se
back (towards the rear)	पीछे	pīchhe
middle	बीच (m)	bīch
in the middle	बीच में	bīch men
at the side	कोने में	kone men
everywhere (adv)	सभी	sabhī
around (in all directions)	आस-पास	ās-pās
from inside	अंदर से	andar se

somewhere (to go)	कहीं	kahīn
straight (directly)	सीधे	sīdhe
back (e.g., come ~)	वापस	vāpas
from anywhere	कहीं से भी	kahīn se bhī
from somewhere	कहीं से	kahīn se
firstly (adv)	पहले	pahale
secondly (adv)	दूसरा	dūsara
thirdly (adv)	तीसरा	tīsara
suddenly (adv)	अचानक	achānak
at first (in the beginning)	शुरू में	shurū men
for the first time	पहली बार	pahalī bār
long before …	बहुत समय पहले …	bahut samay pahale …
anew (over again)	नई शुरूआत	naī shurūāt
for good (adv)	हमेशा के लिए	hamesha ke lie
never (adv)	कभी नहीं	kabhī nahin
again (adv)	फिर से	fir se
now (adv)	अब	ab
often (adv)	अकसर	akasar
then (adv)	तब	tab
urgently (quickly)	तत्काल	tatkāl
usually (adv)	आमतौर पर	āmataur par
by the way, …	प्रसंगवश	prasangavash
possible (that is ~)	मुमकिन	mumakin
probably (adv)	संभव	sambhav
maybe (adv)	शायद	shāyad
besides …	इस के अलावा	is ke alāva
that's why …	इस लिए	is lie
in spite of …	फिर भी …	fir bhī …
thanks to …	… की मेहरबानी से	… kī meharabānī se
what (pron.)	क्या	kya
that (conj.)	कि	ki
something	कुछ	kuchh
anything (something)	कुछ भी	kuchh bhī
nothing	कुछ नहीं	kuchh nahin
who (pron.)	कौन	kaun
someone	कोई	koī
somebody	कोई	koī
nobody	कोई नहीं	koī nahin
nowhere (a voyage to ~)	कहीं नहीं	kahīn nahin
nobody's	किसी का नहीं	kisī ka nahin
somebody's	किसी का	kisī ka
so (I'm ~ glad)	कितना	kitana
also (as well)	भी	bhī
too (as well)	भी	bhī

6. Function words. Adverbs. Part 2

Why?	क्यों?	kyon?
for some reason	किसी कारणवश	kisī kāranavash
because ...	क्यों कि ...	kyon ki ...
for some purpose	किसी वजह से	kisī vajah se

and	और	aur
or	या	ya
but	लेकिन	lekin
for (e.g., ~ me)	के लिए	ke lie

too (~ many people)	ज़्यादा	zyāda
only (exclusively)	सिर्फ़	sirf
exactly (adv)	ठीक	thīk
about (more or less)	करीब	karīb

approximately (adv)	लगभग	lagabhag
approximate (adj)	अनुमानित	anumānit
almost (adv)	करीब	karīb
the rest	बाक़ी	bāqī

each (adj)	हर एक	har ek
any (no matter which)	कोई	koī
many, much (a lot of)	बहुत	bahut
many people	बहुत लोग	bahut log
all (everyone)	सभी	sabhī

in return for ...	... के बदले में	... ke badale men
in exchange (adv)	की जगह	kī jagah
by hand (made)	हाथ से	hāth se
hardly (negative opinion)	शायद ही	shāyad hī

probably (adv)	शायद	shāyad
on purpose (intentionally)	जानबूझकर	jānabūjhakar
by accident (adv)	संयोगवश	sanyogavash

very (adv)	बहुत	bahut
for example (adv)	उदाहरण के लिए	udāharan ke lie
between	के बीच	ke bīch
among	में	men
so much (such a lot)	इतना	itana
especially (adv)	ख़ासतौर पर	khāsataur par

NUMBERS. MISCELLANEOUS

T&P Books Publishing

0 zero	ज़ीरो	zīro
1 one	एक	ek
2 two	दो	do
3 three	तीन	tīn
4 four	चार	chār
5 five	पाँच	pānch
6 six	छह	chhah
7 seven	सात	sāt
8 eight	आठ	āth
9 nine	नौ	nau
10 ten	दस	das
11 eleven	ग्यारह	gyārah
12 twelve	बारह	bārah
13 thirteen	तेरह	terah
14 fourteen	चौदह	chaudah
15 fifteen	पन्द्रह	pandrah
16 sixteen	सोलह	solah
17 seventeen	सत्रह	satrah
18 eighteen	अठारह	athārah
19 nineteen	उन्नीस	unnīs
20 twenty	बीस	bīs
21 twenty-one	इक्कीस	ikkīs
22 twenty-two	बाईस	baīs
23 twenty-three	तेईस	teīs
30 thirty	तीस	tīs
31 thirty-one	इकतीस	ikattīs
32 thirty-two	बत्तीस	battīs
33 thirty-three	तैंतीस	taintīs
40 forty	चालीस	chālīs
41 forty-one	इक्तालीस	iktālīs
42 forty-two	बयालीस	bayālīs
43 forty-three	तैंतालीस	taintālīs
50 fifty	पचास	pachās
51 fifty-one	इक्यावन	ikyāvan
52 fifty-two	बावन	bāvan
53 fifty-three	तिरपन	tirapan
60 sixty	साठ	sāth

61 sixty-one	इकसठ	ikasath
62 sixty-two	बासठ	bāsath
63 sixty-three	तिरसठ	tirasath

70 seventy	सत्तर	sattar
71 seventy-one	इकहत्तर	ikahattar
72 seventy-two	बहत्तर	bahattar
73 seventy-three	तिहत्तर	tihattar

80 eighty	अस्सी	assī
81 eighty-one	इक्यासी	ikyāsī
82 eighty-two	बयासी	bayāsī
83 eighty-three	तिरासी	tirāsī

90 ninety	नब्बे	nabbe
91 ninety-one	इक्यानवे	ikyānave
92 ninety-two	बानवे	bānave
93 ninety-three	तिरानवे	tirānave

8. Cardinal numbers. Part 2

100 one hundred	सौ	sau
200 two hundred	दो सौ	do sau
300 three hundred	तीन सौ	tīn sau
400 four hundred	चार सौ	chār sau
500 five hundred	पाँच सौ	pānch sau

600 six hundred	छह सौ	chhah sau
700 seven hundred	सात सो	sāt so
800 eight hundred	आठ सौ	āth sau
900 nine hundred	नौ सौ	nau sau

1000 one thousand	एक हज़ार	ek hazār
2000 two thousand	दो हज़ार	do hazār
3000 three thousand	तीन हज़ार	tīn hazār
10000 ten thousand	दस हज़ार	das hazār
one hundred thousand	एक लाख	ek lākh
million	दस लाख (m)	das lākh
billion	अरब (m)	arab

9. Ordinal numbers

first (adj)	पहला	pahala
second (adj)	दूसरा	dūsara
third (adj)	तीसरा	tīsara
fourth (adj)	चौथा	chautha
fifth (adj)	पाँचवाँ	pānchavān
sixth (adj)	छठा	chhatha

seventh (adj)	सातवाँ	sātavān
eighth (adj)	आठवाँ	āthavān
ninth (adj)	नौवाँ	nauvān
tenth (adj)	दसवाँ	dasavān

COLOURS. UNITS OF MEASUREMENT

T&P Books Publishing

10. Colors

color	रंग (m)	rang
shade (tint)	रंग (m)	rang
hue	रंग (m)	rang
rainbow	इन्द्रधनुष (f)	indradhanush
white (adj)	सफ़ेद	safed
black (adj)	काला	kāla
gray (adj)	धूसर	dhūsar
green (adj)	हरा	hara
yellow (adj)	पीला	pīla
red (adj)	लाल	lāl
blue (adj)	नीला	nīla
light blue (adj)	हल्का नीला	halka nīla
pink (adj)	गुलाबी	gulābī
orange (adj)	नारंगी	nārangī
violet (adj)	बैंगनी	bainganī
brown (adj)	भूरा	bhūra
golden (adj)	सुनहरा	sunahara
silvery (adj)	चाँदी-जैसा	chāndī-jaisa
beige (adj)	हल्का भूरा	halka bhūra
cream (adj)	क्रीम	krīm
turquoise (adj)	फ़ीरोज़ी	fīrozī
cherry red (adj)	चेरी जैसा लाल	cherī jaisa lāl
lilac (adj)	हल्का बैंगनी	halka bainganī
crimson (adj)	गहरा लाल	gahara lāl
light (adj)	हल्का	halka
dark (adj)	गहरा	gahara
bright, vivid (adj)	चमकीला	chamakīla
colored (pencils)	रंगीन	rangīn
color (e.g., ~ film)	रंगीन	rangīn
black-and-white (adj)	काला-सफ़ेद	kāla-safed
plain (one-colored)	एक रंग का	ek rang ka
multicolored (adj)	बहुरंगी	bahurangī

11. Units of measurement

weight	वज़न (m)	vazan
length	लम्बाई (f)	lambaī

width	चौड़ाई (f)	chauraī
height	ऊंचाई (f)	ūnchaī
depth	गहराई (f)	gaharaī
volume	घनत्व (f)	ghanatv
area	क्षेत्रफल (m)	kshetrafal

gram	ग्राम (m)	grām
milligram	मिलीग्राम (m)	milīgrām
kilogram	किलोग्राम (m)	kilogrām
ton	टन (m)	tan
pound	पौण्ड (m)	paund
ounce	औन्स (m)	auns

meter	मीटर (m)	mītar
millimeter	मिलीमीटर (m)	milīmītar
centimeter	सेंटीमीटर (m)	sentīmītar
kilometer	किलोमीटर (m)	kilomītar
mile	मील (m)	mīl

inch	इंच (m)	inch
foot	फुट (m)	fut
yard	गॅज (m)	gaj

square meter	वर्ग मीटर (m)	varg mītar
hectare	हेक्टेयर (m)	hekteyar
liter	लीटर (m)	lītar
degree	डिग्री (m)	digrī
volt	वोल्ट (m)	volt
ampere	ऐम्पेयर (m)	aimpeyar
horsepower	अश्व शक्ति (f)	ashv shakti

quantity	मात्रा (f)	mātra
a little bit of …	कुछ …	kuchh …
half	आधा (m)	ādha
dozen	दर्जन (m)	darjan
piece (item)	टुकड़ा (m)	tukara

| size | माप (m) | māp |
| scale (map ~) | पैमाना (m) | paimāna |

minimal (adj)	न्यूनतम	nyūnatam
the smallest (adj)	सब से छोटा	sab se chhota
medium (adj)	मध्य	madhy
maximal (adj)	अधिकतम	adhikatam
the largest (adj)	सबसे बड़ा	sabase bara

12. Containers

| canning jar (glass ~) | शीशी (f) | shīshī |
| can | डिब्बा (m) | dibba |

bucket	बाल्टी (f)	bāltī
barrel	पीपा (m)	pīpa
wash basin (e.g., plastic ~)	चिलमची (f)	chilamachī
tank (100L water ~)	कुण्ड (m)	kund
hip flask	फ्लास्क (m)	flāsk
jerrycan	जेरिकैन (m)	jerikain
tank (e.g., tank car)	टंकी (f)	tankī
mug	मग (m)	mag
cup (of coffee, etc.)	प्याली (f)	pyālī
saucer	सॉसर (m)	sosar
glass (tumbler)	गिलास (m)	gilās
wine glass	वाइन गिलास (m)	vain gilās
stock pot (soup pot)	सॉसपैन (m)	sosapain
bottle (~ of wine)	बोतल (f)	botal
neck (of the bottle, etc.)	गला (m)	gala
carafe (decanter)	जग (m)	jag
pitcher	सुराही (f)	surāhī
vessel (container)	बरतन (m)	baratan
pot (crock, stoneware ~)	घड़ा (m)	ghara
vase	फूलदान (m)	fūladān
bottle (perfume ~)	शीशी (f)	shīshī
vial, small bottle	शीशी (f)	shīshī
tube (of toothpaste)	ट्यूब (m)	tyūb
sack (bag)	थैला (m)	thaila
bag (paper ~, plastic ~)	थैली (f)	thailī
pack (of cigarettes, etc.)	पैकेट (f)	paiket
box (e.g., shoebox)	डिब्बा (m)	dibba
crate	डिब्बा (m)	dibba
basket	टोकरी (f)	tokarī

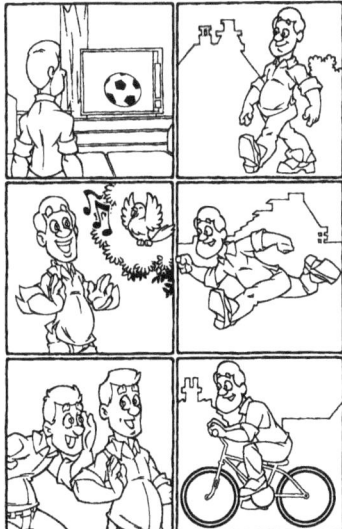

MAIN VERBS

T&P Books Publishing

13. The most important verbs. Part 1

to advise (vt)	सलाह देना	salāh dena
to agree (say yes)	राज़ी होना	rāzī hona
to answer (vi, vt)	जवाब देना	javāb dena
to apologize (vi)	माफ़ी मांगना	māfī māngana
to arrive (vi)	पहुँचना	pahunchana
to ask (~ oneself)	पूछना	pūchhana
to ask (~ sb to do sth)	मांगना	māngana
to be (vi)	होना	hona
to be afraid	डरना	darana
to be hungry	भूख लगना	bhūkh lagana
to be interested in ...	रुचि लेना	ruchi lena
to be needed	आवश्यक होना	āvashyak hona
to be surprised	हैरान होना	hairān hona
to be thirsty	प्यास लगना	pyās lagana
to begin (vt)	शुरू करना	shurū karana
to belong to ...	स्वामी होना	svāmī hona
to boast (vi)	डींग मारना	dīng mārana
to break (split into pieces)	तोड़ना	torana
to call (~ for help)	बुलाना	bulāna
can (v aux)	सकना	sakana
to catch (vt)	पकड़ना	pakarana
to change (vt)	बदलना	badalana
to choose (select)	चुनना	chunana
to come down (the stairs)	उतरना	utarana
to compare (vt)	तुलना करना	tulana karana
to complain (vi, vt)	शिकायत करना	shikāyat karana
to confuse (mix up)	गड़बड़ा जाना	garabara jāna
to continue (vt)	जारी रखना	jārī rakhana
to control (vt)	नियंत्रित करना	niyantrit karana
to cook (dinner)	खाना बनाना	khāna banāna
to cost (vt)	दाम होना	dām hona
to count (add up)	गिनना	ginana
to count on ...	भरोसा रखना	bharosa rakhana
to create (vt)	बनाना	banāna
to cry (weep)	रोना	rona

14. The most important verbs. Part 2

to deceive (vi, vt)	धोखा देना	dhokha dena
to decorate (tree, street)	सजाना	sajāna
to defend (a country, etc.)	रक्षा करना	raksha karana
to demand (request firmly)	माँगना	māngana
to dig (vt)	खोदना	khodana
to discuss (vt)	चर्चा करना	charcha karana
to do (vt)	करना	karana
to doubt (have doubts)	शक करना	shak karana
to drop (let fall)	गिराना	girāna
to enter (room, house, etc.)	अंदर आना	andar āna
to exist (vi)	होना	hona
to expect (foresee)	उम्मीद करना	ummīd karana
to explain (vt)	समझाना	samajhāna
to fall (vi)	गिरना	girana
to find (vt)	ढूढ़ना	dhūrhana
to finish (vt)	ख़त्म करना	khatm karana
to fly (vi)	उड़ना	urana
to follow ... (come after)	पीछे चलना	pīchhe chalana
to forget (vi, vt)	भूलना	bhūlana
to forgive (vt)	क्षमा करना	kshama karana
to give (vt)	देना	dena
to give a hint	इशारा करना	ishāra karana
to go (on foot)	जाना	jāna
to go for a swim	तैरना	tairana
to go out (for dinner, etc.)	बाहर जाना	bāhar jāna
to guess (the answer)	अंदाज़ा लगाना	andāza lagāna
to have (vt)	होना	hona
to have breakfast	नाश्ता करना	nāshta karana
to have dinner	रात्रिभोज करना	rātribhoj karana
to have lunch	दोपहर का भोजन करना	dopahar ka bhojan karana
to hear (vt)	सुनना	sunana
to help (vt)	मदद करना	madad karana
to hide (vt)	छिपाना	chhipāna
to hope (vi, vt)	आशा करना	āsha karana
to hunt (vi, vt)	शिकार करना	shikār karana
to hurry (vi)	जल्दी करना	jaldī karana

15. The most important verbs. Part 3

to inform (vt)	खबर देना	khabar dena
to insist (vi, vt)	आग्रह करना	āgrah karana

to insult (vt)	अपमान करना	apamān karana
to invite (vt)	आमंत्रित करना	āmantrit karana
to joke (vi)	मज़ाक करना	mazāk karana
to keep (vt)	रखना	rakhana
to keep silent	चुप रहना	chup rahana
to kill (vt)	मार डालना	mār dālana
to know (sb)	जानना	jānana
to know (sth)	मालूम होना	mālūm hona
to laugh (vi)	हंसना	hansana
to liberate (city, etc.)	आज़ाद करना	āzād karana
to like (I like …)	पसंद करना	pasand karana
to look for … (search)	तलाश करना	talāsh karana
to love (sb)	प्यार करना	pyār karana
to make a mistake	गलती करना	galatī karana
to manage, to run	प्रबंधन करना	prabandhan karana
to mean (signify)	अर्थ होना	arth hona
to mention (talk about)	उल्लेख करना	ullekh karana
to miss (school, etc.)	ग़ैर-हाज़िर होना	gair-hāzir hona
to notice (see)	देखना	dekhana
to object (vi, vt)	एतराज़ करना	etarāz karana
to observe (see)	देखना	dekhana
to open (vt)	खोलना	kholana
to order (meal, etc.)	ऑर्डर करना	ordar karana
to order (mil.)	हुक्म देना	hukm dena
to own (possess)	मालिक होना	mālik hona
to participate (vi)	भाग लेना	bhāg lena
to pay (vi, vt)	दाम चुकाना	dām chukāna
to permit (vt)	अनुमति देना	anumati dena
to plan (vt)	योजना बनाना	yojana banāna
to play (children)	खेलना	khelana
to pray (vi, vt)	दुआ देना	dua dena
to prefer (vt)	तरजीह देना	tarajīh dena
to promise (vt)	वचन देना	vachan dena
to pronounce (vt)	उच्चारण करना	uchchāran karana
to propose (vt)	प्रस्ताव रखना	prastāv rakhana
to punish (vt)	सज़ा देना	saza dena

16. The most important verbs. Part 4

to read (vi, vt)	पढ़ना	parhana
to recommend (vt)	सिफ़ारिश करना	sifārish karana
to refuse (vi, vt)	इन्कार करना	inkār karana
to regret (be sorry)	अफ़सोस जताना	afasos jatāna
to rent (sth from sb)	किराए पर लेना	kirae par lena

to repeat (say again)	दोहराना	doharāna
to reserve, to book	बुक करना	buk karana
to run (vi)	दौड़ना	daurana
to save (rescue)	बचाना	bachāna
to say (~ thank you)	कहना	kahana
to scold (vt)	डाँटना	dāntana
to see (vt)	देखना	dekhana
to sell (vt)	बेचना	bechana
to send (vt)	भेजना	bhejana
to shoot (vi)	गोली चलाना	golī chalāna
to shout (vi)	चिल्लाना	chillāna
to show (vt)	दिखाना	dikhāna
to sign (document)	हस्ताक्षर करना	hastākshar karana
to sit down (vi)	बैठना	baithana
to smile (vi)	मुस्कुराना	muskurāna
to speak (vi, vt)	बोलना	bolana
to steal (money, etc.)	चुराना	churāna
to stop (for pause, etc.)	रुकना	rukana
to stop (please ~ calling me)	बंद करना	band karana
to study (vt)	पढ़ाई करना	parhaī karana
to swim (vi)	तैरना	tairana
to take (vt)	लेना	lena
to think (vi, vt)	सोचना	sochana
to threaten (vt)	धमकाना	dhamakāna
to touch (with hands)	छूना	chhūna
to translate (vt)	अनुवाद करना	anuvād karana
to trust (vt)	यकीन करना	yakīn karana
to try (attempt)	कोशिश करना	koshish karana
to turn (e.g., ~ left)	मुड़ जाना	mur jāna
to underestimate (vt)	कम मूल्यांकन करना	kam mūlyānkan karana
to understand (vt)	समझना	samajhana
to unite (vt)	संयुक्त करना	sanyukt karana
to wait (vt)	इंतज़ार करना	intazār karana
to want (wish, desire)	चाहना	chāhana
to warn (vt)	चेतावनी देना	chetāvanī dena
to work (vi)	काम करना	kām karana
to write (vt)	लिखना	likhana
to write down	लिख लेना	likh lena

T&P BOOKS

TIME. CALENDAR

T&P Books Publishing

17. Weekdays

Monday	सोमवार (m)	somavār
Tuesday	मंगलवार (m)	mangalavār
Wednesday	बुधवार (m)	budhavār
Thursday	गुरूवार (m)	gurūvār
Friday	शुक्रवार (m)	shukravār
Saturday	शनिवार (m)	shanivār
Sunday	रविवार (m)	ravivār
today (adv)	आज	āj
tomorrow (adv)	कल	kal
the day after tomorrow	परसों	parason
yesterday (adv)	कल	kal
the day before yesterday	परसों	parason
day	दिन (m)	din
working day	कार्यदिवस (m)	kāryadivas
public holiday	सार्वजनिक छुट्टी (f)	sārvajanik chhuttī
day off	छुट्टी का दिन (m)	chhuttī ka din
weekend	संसाहांत (m)	saptāhānt
all day long	सारा दिन	sāra din
the next day (adv)	अगला दिन	agala din
two days ago	दो दिन पहले	do din pahale
the day before	एक दिन पहले	ek din pahale
daily (adj)	दैनिक	dainik
every day (adv)	हर दिन	har din
week	हफ़्ता (f)	hafata
last week (adv)	पिछले हफ़्ते	pichhale hafate
next week (adv)	अगले हफ़्ते	agale hafate
weekly (adj)	समाहिक	saptāhik
every week (adv)	हर हफ़्ते	har hafate
twice a week	हफ़्ते में दो बार	hafate men do bār
every Tuesday	हर मंगलवार को	har mangalavār ko

18. Hours. Day and night

morning	सुबह (m)	subah
in the morning	सुबह में	subah men
noon, midday	दोपहर (m)	dopahar
in the afternoon	दोपहर में	dopahar men
evening	शाम (m)	shām

in the evening	शाम में	shām men
night	रात (f)	rāt
at night	रात में	rāt men
midnight	आधी रात (f)	ādhī rāt

second	सेकन्ड (m)	sekand
minute	मिनट (m)	minat
hour	घंटा (m)	ghanta
half an hour	आधा घंटा	ādha ghanta
a quarter-hour	सवा	sava
fifteen minutes	पंद्रह मीनट	pandrah mīnat
24 hours	24 घंटे (m)	chaubīs ghante

sunrise	सूर्योदय (m)	sūryoday
dawn	सूर्योदय (m)	sūryoday
early morning	प्रातःकाल (m)	prātahkāl
sunset	सूर्यास्त (m)	sūryāst

early in the morning	सुबह-सवेरे	subah-savere
this morning	इस सुबह	is subah
tomorrow morning	कल सुबह	kal subah

this afternoon	आज शाम	āj shām
in the afternoon	दोपहर में	dopahar men
tomorrow afternoon	कल दोपहर	kal dopahar

| tonight (this evening) | आज शाम | āj shām |
| tomorrow night | कल रात | kal rāt |

at 3 o'clock sharp	ठीक तीन बजे में	thīk tīn baje men
about 4 o'clock	लगभग चार बजे	lagabhag chār baje
by 12 o'clock	बारह बजे तक	bārah baje tak

in 20 minutes	बीस मीनट में	bīs mīnat men
in an hour	एक घंटे में	ek ghante men
on time (adv)	ठीक समय पर	thīk samay par

a quarter of ...	पौने ... बजे	paune ... baje
within an hour	एक घंटे के अंदर	ek ghante ke andar
every 15 minutes	हर पंद्रह मीनट	har pandrah mīnat
round the clock	दिन-रात (m pl)	din-rāt

19. Months. Seasons

January	जनवरी (m)	janavarī
February	फ़रवरी (m)	faravarī
March	मार्च (m)	mārch
April	अप्रैल (m)	aprail
May	माई (m)	maī
June	जून (m)	jūn

July	जुलाई (m)	julaī
August	अगस्त (m)	agast
September	सितम्बर (m)	sitambar
October	अक्तूबर (m)	aktūbar
November	नवम्बर (m)	navambar
December	दिसम्बर (m)	disambar
spring	वसन्त (m)	vasant
in spring	वसन्त में	vasant men
spring (as adj)	वसन्त	vasant
summer	गरमी (f)	garamī
in summer	गरमियों में	garamiyon men
summer (as adj)	गरमी	garamī
fall	शरद (m)	sharad
in fall	शरद में	sharad men
fall (as adj)	शरद	sharad
winter	सर्दी (f)	sardī
in winter	सर्दियों में	sardiyon men
winter (as adj)	सर्दी	sardī
month	महीना (m)	mahīna
this month	इस महीने	is mahīne
next month	अगले महीने	agale mahīne
last month	पिछले महीने	pichhale mahīne
a month ago	एक महीने पहले	ek mahīne pahale
in a month (a month later)	एक महीने में	ek mahīne men
in 2 months (2 months later)	दो महीने में	do mahīne men
the whole month	पूरे महीने	pūre mahīne
all month long	पूरे महीने	pūre mahīne
monthly (~ magazine)	मासिक	māsik
monthly (adv)	हर महीने	har mahīne
every month	हर महीने	har mahīne
twice a month	महीने में दो बार	mahine men do bār
year	वर्ष (m)	varsh
this year	इस साल	is sāl
next year	अगले साल	agale sāl
last year	पिछले साल	pichhale sāl
a year ago	एक साल पहले	ek sāl pahale
in a year	एक साल में	ek sāl men
in two years	दो साल में	do sāl men
the whole year	पूरा साल	pūra sāl
all year long	पूरा साल	pūra sāl
every year	हर साल	har sāl
annual (adj)	वार्षिक	vārshik

| annually (adv) | वार्षिक | vārshik |
| 4 times a year | साल में चार बार | sāl men chār bār |

date (e.g., today's ~)	तारीख़ (f)	tārīkh
date (e.g., ~ of birth)	तारीख़ (f)	tārīkh
calendar	कैलेन्डर (m)	kailendar

half a year	आधे वर्ष (m)	ādhe varsh
six months	छमाही (f)	chhamāhī
season (summer, etc.)	मौसम (m)	mausam
century	शताबदी (f)	shatābadī

TRAVEL. HOTEL

T&P Books Publishing

20. Trip. Travel

tourism, travel	पर्यटन (m)	paryatan
tourist	पर्यटक (m)	paryatak
trip, voyage	यात्रा (f)	yātra
adventure	जाँबाज़ी (f)	jānbāzī
trip, journey	यात्रा (f)	yātra
vacation	छुट्टी (f)	chhuttī
to be on vacation	छुट्टी पर होना	chhuttī par hona
rest	आराम (m)	ārām
train	रेलगाड़ी, ट्रेन (f)	relagārī, tren
by train	रैलगाड़ी से	railagārī se
airplane	विमान (m)	vimān
by airplane	विमान से	vimān se
by car	कार से	kār se
by ship	जहाज़ पर	jahāz par
luggage	सामान (m)	sāmān
suitcase	सूटकेस (m)	sūtakes
luggage cart	सामान के लिये गाड़ी (f)	sāmān ke liye gārī
passport	पासपोर्ट (m)	pāsaport
visa	वीज़ा (m)	vīza
ticket	टिकट (m)	tikat
air ticket	हवाई टिकट (m)	havaī tikat
guidebook	गाइडबुक (f)	gaidabuk
map (tourist ~)	नक्शा (m)	naksha
area (rural ~)	क्षेत्र (m)	kshetr
place, site	स्थान (m)	sthān
exotica (n)	विचित्र वस्तुएं	vichitr vastuen
exotic (adj)	विचित्र	vichitr
amazing (adj)	अजीब	ajīb
group	समूह (m)	samūh
excursion, sightseeing tour	पर्यटन (f)	paryatan
guide (person)	गाइड (m)	gaid

21. Hotel

hotel	होटल (f)	hotal
motel	मोटल (m)	motal

three-star (~ hotel)	तीन सितारा	tīn sitāra
five-star	पाँच सितारा	pānch sitāra
to stay (in a hotel, etc.)	ठहरना	thaharana

room	कमरा (m)	kamara
single room	एक पलंग का कमरा (m)	ek palang ka kamara
double room	दो पलंगों का कमरा (m)	do palangon ka kamara
to book a room	कमरा बुक करना	kamara buk karana

| half board | हाफ़-बोर्ड (m) | hāf-bord |
| full board | फ़ुल-बोर्ड (m) | ful-bord |

with bath	स्नानघर के साथ	snānaghar ke sāth
with shower	शॉवर के साथ	shovar ke sāth
satellite television	सैटेलाइट टेलीविज़न (m)	saitelait telīvizan
air-conditioner	एयर-कंडिशनर (m)	eyar-kandishanar
towel	तौलिया (f)	tauliya
key	चाबी (f)	chābī

administrator	मैनेजर (m)	mainejar
chambermaid	चैमबरमैड (f)	chaimabaramaid
porter, bellboy	कुली (m)	kulī
doorman	दरबान (m)	darabān

restaurant	रेस्टराँ (m)	restarān
pub, bar	बार (m)	bār
breakfast	नाश्ता (m)	nāshta
dinner	रात्रिभोज (m)	rātribhoj
buffet	बुफ़े (m)	bufe

| lobby | लॉबी (f) | lobī |
| elevator | लिफ़्ट (m) | lift |

| DO NOT DISTURB | परेशान न करें | pareshān na karen |
| NO SMOKING | धूम्रपान निषेधा। | dhumrapān nishedh! |

22. Sightseeing

monument	स्मारक (m)	smārak
fortress	किला (m)	kila
palace	भवन (m)	bhavan
castle	महल (m)	mahal
tower	मीनार (m)	mīnār
mausoleum	समाधि (f)	samādhi

architecture	वस्तुशाला (m)	vastushāla
medieval (adj)	मध्ययुगीय	madhayayugīy
ancient (adj)	प्राचीन	prāchīn
national (adj)	राष्ट्रीय	rāshtrīy
famous (monument, etc.)	मशहूर	mashhūr

tourist	पर्यटक (m)	paryatak
guide (person)	गाइड (m)	gaid
excursion, sightseeing tour	पर्यटन यात्रा (m)	paryatan yātra
to show (vt)	दिखाना	dikhāna
to tell (vt)	बताना	batāna
to find (vt)	ढूँढना	dhūnrhana
to get lost (lose one's way)	खो जाना	kho jāna
map (e.g., subway ~)	नक्शा (m)	naksha
map (e.g., city ~)	नक्शा (m)	naksha
souvenir, gift	यादगार (m)	yādagār
gift shop	गिफ्ट शॉप (f)	gift shop
to take pictures	फ़ोटो खींचना	foto khīnchana
to have one's picture taken	अपना फ़ोटो खिंचवाना	apana foto khinchavāna

T&P BOOKS

TRANSPORTATION

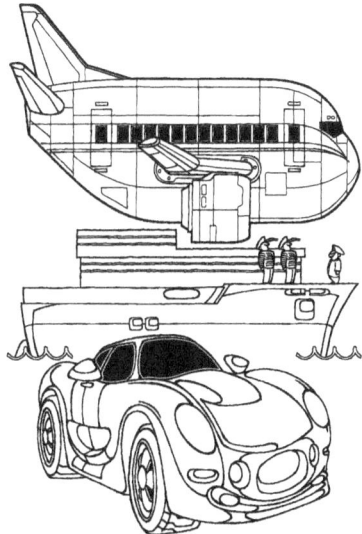

T&P Books Publishing

23. Airport

airport	हवाई अड्डा (m)	havaī adda
airplane	विमान (m)	vimān
airline	हवाई कम्पनी (f)	havaī kampanī
air traffic controller	हवाई यातायात नियंत्रक (m)	havaī yātāyāt niyantrak
departure	प्रस्थान (m)	prasthān
arrival	आगमन (m)	āgaman
to arrive (by plane)	पहुंचना	pahunchana
departure time	उड़ान का समय (m)	urān ka samay
arrival time	आगमन का समय (m)	āgaman ka samay
to be delayed	देर से आना	der se āna
flight delay	उड़ान देरी (f)	urān derī
information board	सूचना बोर्ड (m)	sūchana bord
information	सूचना (f)	sūchana
to announce (vt)	घोषणा करना	ghoshana karana
flight (e.g., next ~)	फ्लाइट (f)	flait
customs	सीमाशुल्क कार्यालय (m)	sīmāshulk kāryālay
customs officer	सीमाशुल्क अधिकारी (m)	sīmāshulk adhikārī
customs declaration	सीमाशुल्क घोषणा (f)	sīmāshulk ghoshana
to fill out the declaration	सीमाशुल्क घोषणा भरना	sīmāshulk ghoshana bharana
passport control	पास्पोर्ट जांच (f)	pāsport jānch
luggage	सामान (m)	sāmān
hand luggage	दस्ती सामान (m)	dastī sāmān
luggage cart	सामान के लिये गाड़ी (f)	sāmān ke liye gārī
landing	विमानारोहण (m)	vimānārohan
landing strip	विमानारोहण मार्ग (m)	vimānārohan mārg
to land (vi)	उतरना	utarana
airstairs	सीढ़ी (f)	sīrhī
check-in	चेक-इन (m)	chek-in
check-in counter	चेक-इन डेस्क (m)	chek-in desk
to check-in (vi)	चेक-इन करना	chek-in karana
boarding pass	बोर्डिंग पास (m)	bording pās
departure gate	प्रस्थान गेट (m)	prasthān get
transit	पारवहन (m)	pāravahan

to wait (vt)	इंतज़ार करना	intazār karana
departure lounge	प्रतीक्षालय (m)	pratīkshālay
to see off	विदा करना	vida karana
to say goodbye	विदा कहना	vida kahana

24. Airplane

airplane	विमान (m)	vimān
air ticket	हवाई टिकट (m)	havaī tikat
airline	हवाई कम्पनी (f)	havaī kampanī
airport	हवाई अड्डा (m)	havaī adda
supersonic (adj)	पराध्वनिक	parādhvanik
captain	कसान (m)	kaptān
crew	वैमानिक दल (m)	vaimānik dal
pilot	विमान चालक (m)	vimān chālak
flight attendant (fem.)	एयर होस्टस (f)	eyar hostas
navigator	नैवीगेटर (m)	naivīgetar
wings	पंख (m pl)	pankh
tail	पूँछ (f)	pūnchh
cockpit	कॉकपिट (m)	kokapit
engine	इंजन (m)	injan
undercarriage (landing gear)	हवाई जहाज़ पहिये (m)	havaī jahāz pahiye
turbine	टरबाइन (f)	tarabain
propeller	प्रोपेलर (m)	propelar
black box	ब्लैक बॉक्स (m)	blaik boks
yoke (control column)	कंट्रोल कॉलम (m)	kantrol kolam
fuel	ईंधन (m)	īndhan
safety card	सुरक्षा-पत्र (m)	suraksha-patr
oxygen mask	ऑक्सीजन मास्क (m)	oksījan māsk
uniform	वर्दी (f)	vardī
life vest	बचाव पेटी (f)	bachāv petī
parachute	पैराशूट (m)	pairāshūt
takeoff	उड़ान (m)	urān
to take off (vi)	उड़ना	urana
runway	उड़ान पट्टी (f)	urān pattī
visibility	दृश्यता (f)	drshyata
flight (act of flying)	उड़ान (m)	urān
altitude	ऊंचाई (f)	ūnchaī
air pocket	वायु-पॉकेट (m)	vāyu-poket
seat	सीट (f)	sīt
headphones	हेडफ़ोन (m)	hedafon
folding tray (tray table)	ट्रे टेबल (f)	tre tebal

| airplane window | हवाई जहाज़ की खिड़की (f) | havaī jahāz kī khirakī |
| aisle | गलियारा (m) | galiyāra |

25. Train

train	रेलगाड़ी, ट्रेन (f)	relagāṛī, tren
commuter train	लोकल ट्रेन (f)	lokal tren
express train	तेज़ रेलगाड़ी (f)	tez relagāṛī
diesel locomotive	डीज़ल रेलगाड़ी (f)	dīzal relagāṛī
steam locomotive	स्टीम इंजन (f)	stīm injan

| passenger car | कोच (f) | koch |
| dining car | डाइनर (f) | dainar |

rails	पटरियाँ (f)	patariyān
railroad	रेलवे (f)	relave
railway tie	पटरियाँ (f)	patariyān

platform (railway ~)	प्लेटफार्म (m)	pletaform
track (~ 1, 2, etc.)	प्लेटफार्म (m)	pletaform
semaphore	सिग्नल (m)	signal
station	स्टेशन (m)	steshan

engineer (train driver)	इंजन ड्राइवर (m)	injan draivar
porter (of luggage)	कुली (m)	kulī
car attendant	कोच एटेंडेंट (m)	koch etendent
passenger	मुसाफिर (m)	musāfir
conductor (ticket inspector)	टीटी (m)	ṭīṭī

| corridor (in train) | गलियारा (m) | galiyāra |
| emergency brake | आपात ब्रेक (m) | āpāt brek |

compartment	डिब्बा (m)	dibba
berth	बर्थ (f)	barth
upper berth	ऊपरी बर्थ (f)	ūparī barth
lower berth	नीचली बर्थ (f)	nīchalī barth
bed linen, bedding	बिस्तर (m)	bistar

ticket	टिकट (m)	tikat
schedule	टाइम टैबुल (m)	taim taibul
information display	सूचना बोर्ड (m)	sūchana bord

to leave, to depart	चले जाना	chale jāna
departure (of train)	रवानगी (f)	ravānagī
to arrive (ab. train)	पहुंचना	pahunchana
arrival	आगमन (m)	āgaman

| to arrive by train | गाड़ी से पहुंचना | gāṛī se pahunchana |
| to get on the train | गाड़ी पकड़ना | gāḍī pakarana |

to get off the train	गाड़ी से उतरना	gārī se utarana
train wreck	दुर्घटनाग्रस्त (f)	durghatanāgrast
steam locomotive	स्टीम इंजन (m)	stīm injan
stoker, fireman	अग्निशामक (m)	agnishāmak
firebox	भट्ठी (f)	bhatthī
coal	कोयला (m)	koyala

26. Ship

ship	जहाज़ (m)	jahāz
vessel	जहाज़ (m)	jahāz
steamship	जहाज़ (m)	jahāz
riverboat	मोटर बोट (m)	motar bot
cruise ship	लाइनर (m)	lainar
cruiser	क्रूज़र (m)	krūzar
yacht	याख्ट (m)	yākht
tugboat	कर्षक पोत (m)	karshak pot
barge	बार्ज (f)	bārj
ferry	फेरी बोट (f)	ferī bot
sailing ship	पाल नाव (f)	pāl nāv
brigantine	बादबानी (f)	bādabānī
ice breaker	हिमभंजक पोत (m)	himabhanjak pot
submarine	पनडुब्बी (f)	panadubbī
boat (flat-bottomed ~)	नाव (m)	nāv
dinghy	किश्ती (f)	kishtī
lifeboat	जीवन रक्षा किश्ती (f)	jīvan raksha kishtī
motorboat	मोटर बोट (m)	motar bot
captain	कसान (m)	kaptān
seaman	मल्लाह (m)	mallāh
sailor	मल्लाह (m)	mallāh
crew	वैमानिक दल (m)	vaimānik dal
boatswain	बोसुन (m)	bosun
ship's boy	बोसुन (m)	bosun
cook	रसोइया (m)	rasoiya
ship's doctor	पोत डाक्टर (m)	pot dāktar
deck	डेक (m)	dek
mast	मस्तूल (m)	mastūl
sail	पाल (m)	pāl
hold	कार्गी (m)	kārgo
bow (prow)	जहाज़ का अगड़ा हिस्सा (m)	jahāz ka agara hissa

stern	जहाज़ का पिछला हिस्सा (m)	jahāz ka pichhala hissa
oar	चप्पू (m)	chappū
screw propeller	जहाज़ की पंखी चलाने का पेंच (m)	jahāz kī pankhī chalāne ka pench
cabin	कैबिन (m)	kaibin
wardroom	मेस (f)	mes
engine room	मशीन-कमरा (m)	mashīn-kamara
bridge	ब्रिज (m)	brij
radio room	रेडियो केबिन (m)	rediyo kebin
wave (radio)	रेडियो तरंग (f)	rediyo tarang
logbook	जहाज़ी रजिस्टर (m)	jahāzī rajistar
spyglass	टेलिस्कोप (m)	teliskop
bell	घंटा (m)	ghanta
flag	झंडा (m)	jhanda
hawser (mooring ~)	रस्सा (m)	rassa
knot (bowline, etc.)	जहाज़ी गांठ (f)	jahāzī gānth
deckrails	रेलिंग (f)	reling
gangway	सीढ़ी (f)	sīrhī
anchor	लंगर (m)	langar
to weigh anchor	लंगर उठाना	langar uthāna
to drop anchor	लंगर डालना	langar dālana
anchor chain	लंगर की ज़जीर (f)	langar kī zajīr
port (harbor)	बंदरगाह (m)	bandaragāh
quay, wharf	घाट (m)	ghāt
to berth (moor)	किनारे लगना	kināre lagana
to cast off	रवाना होना	ravāna hona
trip, voyage	यात्रा (f)	yātra
cruise (sea trip)	जलयात्रा (f)	jalayātra
course (route)	दिशा (f)	disha
route (itinerary)	मार्ग (m)	mārg
fairway (safe water channel)	नाव्य जलपथ (m)	nāvy jalapath
shallows	छिछला पानी (m)	chhichhala pānī
to run aground	छिछले पानी में धसना	chhichhale pānī men dhansana
storm	तूफ़ान (m)	tufān
signal	सिग्नल (m)	signal
to sink (vi)	डूबना	dūbana
SOS (distress signal)	एसओएस	esoes
ring buoy	लाइफ़ ब्वाय (m)	laif bvāy

CITY

T&P Books Publishing

bus	बस (f)	bas
streetcar	ट्रैम (m)	traim
trolley bus	ट्रॉलीबस (f)	trolības
route (of bus, etc.)	मार्ग (m)	mārg
number (e.g., bus ~)	नम्बर (m)	nambar
to go by ...	के माध्यम से जाना	ke mādhyam se jāna
to get on (~ the bus)	सवार होना	savār hona
to get off ...	उतरना	utarana
stop (e.g., bus ~)	बस स्टॉप (m)	bas stop
next stop	अगला स्टॉप (m)	agala stop
terminus	अंतिम स्टेशन (m)	antim steshan
schedule	समय सारणी (f)	samay sāranī
to wait (vt)	इंतज़ार करना	intazār karana
ticket	टिकट (m)	tikat
fare	टिकट का किराया (m)	tikat ka kirāya
cashier (ticket seller)	कैशियर (m)	kaishiyar
ticket inspection	टिकट जाँच (f)	tikat jānch
ticket inspector	कंडक्टर (m)	kandaktar
to be late (for ...)	देर हो जाना	der ho jāna
to miss (~ the train, etc.)	छूट जाना	chhūt jāna
to be in a hurry	जल्दी में रहना	jaldī men rahana
taxi, cab	टैक्सी (m)	taiksī
taxi driver	टैक्सीवाला (m)	taiksīvāla
by taxi	टैक्सी से (m)	taiksī se
taxi stand	टैक्सी स्टैंड (m)	taiksī staind
to call a taxi	टैक्सी बुलाना	taiksī bulāna
to take a taxi	टैक्सी लेना	taiksī lena
traffic	यातायात (f)	yātāyāt
traffic jam	ट्रैफ़िक जाम (m)	traifik jām
rush hour	भीड़ का समय (m)	bhīr ka samay
to park (vi)	पार्क करना	pārk karana
to park (vt)	पार्क करना	pārk karana
parking lot	पार्किंग (f)	pārking
subway	मेट्रो (m)	metro
station	स्टेशन (m)	steshan
to take the subway	मेट्रो लेना	metro lena

| train | रेलगाड़ी, ट्रेन (f) | relagārī, tren |
| train station | स्टेशन (m) | steshan |

28. City. Life in the city

city, town	नगर (m)	nagar
capital city	राजधानी (f)	rājadhānī
village	गांव (m)	gānv

city map	नगर का नक्शा (m)	nagar ka naksha
downtown	नगर का केन्द्र (m)	nagar ka kendr
suburb	उपनगर (m)	upanagar
suburban (adj)	उपनगरिक	upanagarik

outskirts	बाहरी इलाका (m)	bāharī ilāka
environs (suburbs)	इर्दगिर्द के इलाके (m pl)	irdagird ke ilāke
city block	सेक्टर (m)	sektar
residential block (area)	मुहल्ला (m)	muhalla

traffic	यातायात (f)	yātāyāt
traffic lights	यातायात सिग्नल (m)	yātāyāt signal
public transportation	जन परिवहन (m)	jan parivahan
intersection	चौराहा (m)	chaurāha

| crosswalk | ज़ेबरा क्रॉसिंग (f) | zebara krosing |
| pedestrian underpass | पैदल यात्रियों के लिए अंडरपास (f) | paidal yātriyon ke lie andarapās |

to cross (~ the street)	सड़क पार करना	sarak pār karana
pedestrian	पैदल-यात्री (m)	paidal-yātrī
sidewalk	फुटपाथ (m)	futapāth

bridge	पुल (m)	pul
embankment (river walk)	तट (m)	tat
fountain	फौवारा (m)	fauvāra

allée (garden walkway)	छायापथ (f)	chhāyāpath
park	पार्क (m)	pārk
boulevard	चौड़ी सड़क (m)	chaurī sarak
square	मैदान (m)	maidān
avenue (wide street)	मार्ग (m)	mārg
street	सड़क (f)	sarak
side street	गली (f)	galī
dead end	बंद गली (f)	band galī

house	मकान (m)	makān
building	इमारत (f)	imārat
skyscraper	गगनचुंबी भवन (f)	gaganachumbī bhavan

| facade | अगवाड़ा (m) | agavāra |
| roof | छत (f) | chhat |

window	खिड़की (f)	khirakī
arch	मेहराब (m)	meharāb
column	स्तंभ (m)	stambh
corner	कोना (m)	kona

store window	दुकान का शो-केस (m)	dukān ka sho-kes
signboard (store sign, etc.)	साईनबोर्ड (m)	saīnabord
poster	पोस्टर (m)	postar
advertising poster	विज्ञापन पोस्टर (m)	vigyāpan postar
billboard	बिलबोर्ड (m)	bilabord

garbage, trash	कूड़ा (m)	kūra
trashcan (public ~)	कूड़े का डिब्बा (m)	kūre ka dibba
to litter (vi)	कूड़ा-कर्कट डालना	kūra-karkat dālana
garbage dump	डम्पिंग ग्राउंड (m)	damping graund

phone booth	फ़ोन बूथ (m)	fon būth
lamppost	बिजली का खंभा (m)	bijalī ka khambha
bench (park ~)	पार्क-बेंच (f)	pārk-bench

police officer	पुलिसवाला (m)	pulisavāla
police	पुलिस (m)	pulis
beggar	भिखारी (m)	bhikhārī
homeless (n)	बेघर (m)	beghar

29. Urban institutions

store	दुकान (f)	dukān
drugstore, pharmacy	दवाख़ाना (m)	davākhāna
eyeglass store	चश्मे की दुकान (f)	chashme kī dukān
shopping mall	शापिंग मॉल (m)	shoping mol
supermarket	सुपर बाज़ार (m)	supar bāzār

bakery	बेकरी (f)	bekarī
baker	बेकर (m)	bekar
pastry shop	टॉफ़ी की दुकान (f)	tofī kī dukān
grocery store	परचून की दुकान (f)	parachūn kī dukān
butcher shop	गोश्त की दुकान (f)	gosht kī dukān

| produce store | सब्ज़ियों की दुकान (f) | sabziyon kī dukān |
| market | बाज़ार (m) | bāzār |

coffee house	काफ़ी हाउस (m)	kāfī haus
restaurant	रेस्टराँ (m)	restarān
pub, bar	शराबख़ाना (m)	sharābakhāna
pizzeria	पिट्ज़ा की दुकान (f)	pitza kī dukān

hair salon	नाई की दुकान (f)	naī kī dukān
post office	डाकघर (m)	dākaghar
dry cleaners	ड्राइक्लीनर (m)	draiklīnar

photo studio	फ़ोटो की दुकान (f)	foto kī dukān
shoe store	जूते की दुकान (f)	jūte kī dukān
bookstore	किताबों की दुकान (f)	kitābon kī dukān
sporting goods store	खेलकूद की दुकान (f)	khelakūd kī dukān
clothes repair shop	कपड़ों की मरम्मत की दुकान (f)	kaparon kī marammat kī dukān
formal wear rental	कपड़ों को किराए पर देने की दुकान (f)	kaparon ko kirae par dene kī dukān
video rental store	वीडियो रेन्टल दुकान (f)	vīdiyo rental dukān
circus	सर्कस (m)	sarkas
zoo	चिड़ियाघर (m)	chiriyāghar
movie theater	सिनेमाघर (m)	sinemāghar
museum	संग्रहालय (m)	sangrahālay
library	पुस्तकालय (m)	pustakālay
theater	रंगमंच (m)	rangamanch
opera (opera house)	ओपेरा (m)	opera
nightclub	नाईट क्लब (m)	naīt klab
casino	केसिनो (m)	kesino
mosque	मस्जिद (m)	masjid
synagogue	सीनागोग (m)	sīnāgog
cathedral	गिरजाघर (m)	girajāghar
temple	मंदिर (m)	mandir
church	गिरजाघर (m)	girajāghar
college	कॉलेज (m)	kolej
university	विश्वविद्यालय (m)	vishvavidyālay
school	विद्यालय (m)	vidyālay
prefecture	प्रशासक प्रान्त (m)	prashāsak prānt
city hall	सिटी हॉल (m)	sitī hol
hotel	होटल (f)	hotal
bank	बैंक (m)	baink
embassy	दूतावस (m)	dūtāvas
travel agency	पर्यटन आफ़िस (m)	paryatan āfis
information office	पूछताछ कार्यालय (m)	pūchhatāchh kāryālay
currency exchange	मुद्रालय (m)	mudrālay
subway	मेट्रो (m)	metro
hospital	अस्पताल (m)	aspatāl
gas station	पेट्रोल पम्प (f)	petrol pamp
parking lot	पार्किंग (f)	pārking

30. Signs

signboard (store sign, etc.)	साईनबोर्ड (m)	saīnabord
notice (door sign, etc.)	दुकान का साईन (m)	dukān ka saīn

poster	पोस्टर (m)	postar
direction sign	दिशा संकेतक (m)	disha sanketak
arrow (sign)	तीर दिशा संकेतक (m)	tīr disha sanketak

caution	चेतावनी (f)	chetāvanī
warning sign	चेतावनी संकेतक (m)	chetāvanī sanketak
to warn (vt)	चेतावनी देना	chetāvanī dena

rest day (weekly ~)	छुट्टी का दिन (m)	chhuttī ka din
timetable (schedule)	समय सारणी (f)	samay sāranī
opening hours	खुलने का समय (m)	khulane ka samay

WELCOME!	आपका स्वागत है!	āpaka svāgat hai!
ENTRANCE	प्रवेश	pravesh
EXIT	निकास	nikās

PUSH	धक्का दें	dhakka den
PULL	खींचे	khīnche
OPEN	खुला	khula
CLOSED	बंद	band

| WOMEN | औरतों के लिये | auraton ke liye |
| MEN | आदमियों के लिये | ādamiyon ke liye |

| DISCOUNTS | डिस्काउन्ट | diskaunt |
| SALE | सेल | sel |

| NEW! | नया! | naya! |
| FREE | मुफ्त | muft |

ATTENTION!	ध्यान दें!	dhyān den!
NO VACANCIES	कोई जगह खाली नहीं है	koī jagah khālī nahin hai
RESERVED	रिज़र्वड	rizarvad

| ADMINISTRATION | प्रशासन | prashāsan |
| STAFF ONLY | केवल कर्मचारियों के लिए | keval karmachāriyon ke lie |

BEWARE OF THE DOG!	कुत्ते से सावधान!	kutte se sāvadhān!
NO SMOKING	धूम्रपान निषेध!	dhumrapān nishedh!
DO NOT TOUCH!	छूना मना!	chhūna mana!

DANGEROUS	खतरा	khatara
DANGER	खतरा	khatara
HIGH VOLTAGE	उच्च वोल्टेज	uchch voltej

| NO SWIMMING! | तैरना मना! | tairana mana! |
| OUT OF ORDER | ख़राब | kharāb |

FLAMMABLE	ज्वलनशील	jvalanashīl
FORBIDDEN	निषिद्ध	nishiddh
NO TRESPASSING!	प्रवेश निषेध!	pravesh nishedh!
WET PAINT	गीला पेंट	gīla pent

31. Shopping

to buy (purchase)	खरीदना	kharīdana
purchase	खरीदारी (f)	kharīdārī
to go shopping	खरीदारी करने जाना	kharīdārī karane jāna
shopping	खरीदारी (f)	kharīdārī
to be open (ab. store)	खुला होना	khula hona
to be closed	बन्द होना	band hona
footwear, shoes	जूता (m)	jūta
clothes, clothing	पोशाक (m)	poshāk
cosmetics	श्रृंगार-सामग्री (f)	shrrngār-sāmagrī
food products	खाने-पीने की चीज़ें (f pl)	khāne-pīne kī chīzen
gift, present	उपहार (m)	upahār
salesman	बेचनेवाला (m)	bechanevāla
saleswoman	बेचनेवाली (f)	bechanevālī
check out, cash desk	कैश-काउन्टर (m)	kaish-kauntar
mirror	आईना (m)	āīna
counter (store ~)	काउन्टर (m)	kauntar
fitting room	ट्राई करने का कमरा (m)	traī karane ka kamara
to try on	ट्राई करना	traī karana
to fit (ab. dress, etc.)	फिटिंग करना	fiting karana
to like (I like …)	पसंद करना	pasand karana
price	दाम (m)	dām
price tag	प्राइस टैग (m)	prais taig
to cost (vt)	दाम होना	dām hona
How much?	कितना?	kitana?
discount	डिस्काउन्ट (m)	diskaunt
inexpensive (adj)	सस्ता	sasta
cheap (adj)	सस्ता	sasta
expensive (adj)	महंगा	mahanga
It's expensive	यह महंगा है	yah mahanga hai
rental (n)	रेन्टल (m)	rental
to rent (~ a tuxedo)	किराए पर लेना	kirae par lena
credit (trade credit)	क्रेडिट (m)	kredit
on credit (adv)	क्रेडिट पर	kredit par

CLOTHING & ACCESSORIES

T&P Books Publishing

32. Outerwear. Coats

clothes	कपड़े (m)	kapare
outerwear	बाहरी पोशाक (m)	bāharī poshāk
winter clothing	सर्दियों की पोशक (f)	sardiyon kī poshak
coat (overcoat)	ओवरकोट (m)	ovarakot
fur coat	फरकोट (m)	farakot
fur jacket	फ़र की जैकेट (f)	far kī jaiket
down coat	फ़ेदर कोट (m)	fedar kot
jacket (e.g., leather ~)	जैकेट (f)	jaiket
raincoat (trenchcoat, etc.)	बरसाती (f)	barasātī
waterproof (adj)	जलरोधक	jalarodhak

33. Men's & women's clothing

shirt (button shirt)	कमीज़ (f)	kamīz
pants	पैंट (m)	paint
jeans	जीन्स (m)	jīns
suit jacket	कोट (m)	kot
suit	सूट (m)	sūt
dress (frock)	फ़ॉक (f)	frok
skirt	स्कर्ट (f)	skart
blouse	ब्लाऊज़ (f)	blauz
knitted jacket (cardigan, etc.)	कार्डिगन (f)	kārdigan
jacket (of woman's suit)	जैकेट (f)	jaiket
T-shirt	टी-शर्ट (f)	tī-shart
shorts (short trousers)	शोर्ट्स (m pl)	shorts
tracksuit	ट्रैक सूट (m)	traik sūt
bathrobe	बाथ रोब (m)	bāth rob
pajamas	पजामा (m)	pajāma
sweater	सूटर (m)	sūtar
pullover	पुलोवर (m)	pulovar
vest	बण्डी (m)	bandī
tailcoat	टेल-कोट (m)	tel-kot
tuxedo	डिनर-जैकेट (f)	dinar-jaiket
uniform	वर्दी (f)	vardī
workwear	वर्दी (f)	vardī

| overalls | ओवरऑल्स (m) | ovarols |
| coat (e.g., doctor's smock) | कोट (m) | kot |

34. Clothing. Underwear

underwear	अंगवस्त्र (m)	angavastr
undershirt (A-shirt)	बनियान (f)	baniyān
socks	मोज़े (m pl)	moze

nightgown	नाइट गाउन (m)	nait gaun
bra	ब्रा (f)	bra
knee highs (knee-high socks)	घुटनों तक के मोज़े (m)	ghutanon tak ke moze

pantyhose	टाइट्स (m pl)	taits
stockings (thigh highs)	स्टाकिंग (m pl)	stāking
bathing suit	स्विम सूट (m)	svim sūt

35. Headwear

hat	टोपी (f)	topī
fedora	हैट (f)	hait
baseball cap	बैस्बॉल कैप (f)	baisbol kaip
flatcap	फ़्लैट कैप (f)	flait kaip

beret	बेरेट (m)	beret
hood	हुड (m)	hūd
panama hat	पनामा हैट (m)	panāma hait
knit cap (knitted hat)	बुनी हुई टोपी (f)	bunī huī topī

| headscarf | सिर का स्कार्फ़ (m) | sir ka skārf |
| women's hat | महिलाओं की टोपी (f) | mahilaon kī topī |

hard hat	हेलमेट (f)	helamet
garrison cap	पुलिसीया टोपी (f)	pulisīya topī
helmet	हेलमेट (f)	helamet

| derby | बॉलर हैट (m) | bolar hait |
| top hat | टॉप हैट (m) | top hait |

36. Footwear

footwear	पनही (f)	panahī
shoes (men's shoes)	जूते (m pl)	jūte
shoes (women's shoes)	जूते (m pl)	jūte
boots (e.g., cowboy ~)	बूट (m pl)	būt
slippers	चप्पल (f pl)	chappal

tennis shoes (e.g., Nike ~)	टेनिस के जूते (m)	tenis ke jūte
sneakers (e.g., Converse ~)	स्नीकर्स (m)	snīkars
sandals	सैन्डल (f)	saindal
cobbler (shoe repairer)	मोची (m)	mochī
heel	एंडी (f)	erī
pair (of shoes)	जोड़ा (m)	jora
shoestring	जूते का फ़ीता (m)	jūte ka fīta
to lace (vt)	फ़ीता बाँधना	fīta bāndhana
shoehorn	शू-होर्न (m)	shū-horn
shoe polish	बूट-पालिश (m)	būt-pālish

37. Personal accessories

gloves	दस्ताने (m pl)	dastāne
mittens	दस्ताने (m pl)	dastāne
scarf (muffler)	मफ़लर (m)	mafalar
glasses (eyeglasses)	ऐनक (m pl)	ainak
frame (eyeglass ~)	चश्मे का फ़्रेम (m)	chashme ka frem
umbrella	छतरी (f)	chhatarī
walking stick	छड़ी (f)	chharī
hairbrush	ब्रश (m)	brash
fan	पंखा (m)	pankha
tie (necktie)	टाई (f)	taī
bow tie	बो टाई (f)	bo taī
suspenders	पतलून बाँधने का फ़ीता (m)	patalūn bāndhane ka fīta
handkerchief	रूमाल (m)	rūmāl
comb	कंघा (m)	kangha
barrette	बालपिन (f)	bālapin
hairpin	हेयरक्लीप (f)	heyaraklīp
buckle	बकसुआ (m)	bakasua
belt	बेल्ट (m)	belt
shoulder strap	कंधे का पट्टा (m)	kandhe ka patta
bag (handbag)	बैग (m)	baig
purse	पर्स (m)	pars
backpack	बैकपैक (m)	baikapaik

38. Clothing. Miscellaneous

fashion	फ़ैशन (m)	faishan
in vogue (adj)	प्रचलन में	prachalan men

fashion designer	फ़ैशन डिज़ाइनर (m)	faishan dizainar
collar	कॉलर (m)	kolar
pocket	जेब (m)	jeb
pocket (as adj)	जेब	jeb
sleeve	आस्तीन (f)	āstīn
hanging loop	हैंगिंग लूप (f)	hainging lūp
fly (on trousers)	ज़िप (f)	zip
zipper (fastener)	ज़िप (f)	zip
fastener	हुक (m)	huk
button	बटन (m)	batan
buttonhole	बटन का काज (m)	batan ka kāj
to come off (ab. button)	निकल जाना	nikal jāna
to sew (vi, vt)	सीना	sīna
to embroider (vi, vt)	काढ़ना	kārhana
embroidery	कढ़ाई (f)	karhaī
sewing needle	सूई (f)	sūī
thread	धागा (m)	dhāga
seam	सीवन (m)	sīvan
to get dirty (vi)	मैला होना	maila hona
stain (mark, spot)	धब्बा (m)	dhabba
to crease, crumple (vi)	शिकन पड़ जाना	shikan par jāna
to tear, to rip (vt)	फट जाना	fat jāna
clothes moth	कपड़ों के कीड़े (m)	kaparon ke kīre

39. Personal care. Cosmetics

toothpaste	टूथपेस्ट (m)	tūthapest
toothbrush	टूथब्रश (m)	tūthabrash
to brush one's teeth	दांत साफ़ करना	dānt sāf karana
razor	रेज़र (f)	rezar
shaving cream	हजामत का क्रीम (m)	hajāmat ka krīm
to shave (vi)	शेव करना	shev karana
soap	साबुन (m)	sābun
shampoo	शैम्पू (m)	shaimpū
scissors	कैंची (f pl)	kainchī
nail file	नाख़ून घिसनी (f)	nākhūn ghisanī
nail clippers	नाख़ून कतरनी (f)	nākhūn kataranī
tweezers	ट्वीज़र्स (f)	tvīzars
cosmetics	श्रृंगार-सामग्री (f)	shrrngār-sāmagrī
face mask	चेहरे का लेप (m)	chehare ka lep
manicure	मैनीक्योर (m)	mainīkyor
to have a manicure	मैनीक्योर करवाना	mainīkyor karavāna
pedicure	पेडिक्यूर (m)	pedikyūr

make-up bag	श्रृंगार थैली (f)	shrrngār thailī
face powder	पाउडर (m)	paudar
powder compact	कॉम्पैक्ट पाउडर (m)	kompaikt paudar
blusher	ब्लशर (m)	blashar
perfume (bottled)	ख़ुशबू (f)	khushabū
toilet water (lotion)	टॉयलेट वॉटर (m)	tāyalet votar
lotion	लोशन (m)	loshan
cologne	कोलोन (m)	kolon
eyeshadow	आई-शैडो (m)	āī-shaido
eyeliner	आई-पेंसिल (f)	āī-pensil
mascara	मस्कारा (m)	maskāra
lipstick	लिपस्टिक (m)	lipastik
nail polish, enamel	नेल पॉलिश (f)	nel polish
hair spray	हेयर स्प्रे (m)	heyar spre
deodorant	डिओडरेन्ट (m)	diodarent
cream	क्रीम (m)	krīm
face cream	चेहरे की क्रीम (f)	chehare kī krīm
hand cream	हाथ की क्रीम (f)	hāth kī krīm
anti-wrinkle cream	एंटी रिंकल क्रीम (f)	entī rinkal krīm
day (as adj)	दिन का	din ka
night (as adj)	रात का	rāt ka
tampon	टैम्पन (m)	taimpan
toilet paper (toilet roll)	टॉयलेट पेपर (m)	toyalet pepar
hair dryer	हेयर ड्रायर (m)	heyar drāyar

40. Watches. Clocks

watch (wristwatch)	घड़ी (f pl)	gharī
dial	डायल (m)	dāyal
hand (of clock, watch)	सुई (f)	suī
metal watch band	धातु से बनी घड़ी का पट्टा (m)	dhātu se banī gharī ka patta
watch strap	घड़ी का पट्टा (m)	gharī ka patta
battery	बैटरी (f)	baiterī
to be dead (battery)	ख़त्म हो जाना	khatm ho jāna
to change a battery	बैटरी बदलना	baiterī badalana
to run fast	तेज़ चलना	tez chalana
to run slow	धीमी चलना	dhīmī chalana
wall clock	दीवार-घड़ी (f pl)	dīvār-gharī
hourglass	रेत-घड़ी (f pl)	ret-gharī
sundial	सूरज-घड़ी (f pl)	sūraj-gharī
alarm clock	अलार्म घड़ी (f)	alārm gharī
watchmaker	घड़ीसाज़ (m)	gharīsāz
to repair (vt)	मरम्मत करना	marammat karana

EVERYDAY EXPERIENCE

T&P Books Publishing

money	पैसा (m pl)	paisa
currency exchange	मुद्रा विनिमय (m)	mudra vinimay
exchange rate	विनिमय दर (m)	vinimay dar
ATM	एटीएम (m)	eṭīem
coin	सिक्का (m)	sikka
dollar	डॉलर (m)	dolar
euro	यूरो (m)	yūro
lira	लीरा (f)	līra
Deutschmark	डचमार्क (m)	dachamārk
franc	फ्रांक (m)	frānk
pound sterling	पाउन्ड स्टरलिंग (m)	paund staraling
yen	येन (m)	yen
debt	कर्ज़ (m)	karz
debtor	क़र्ज़दार (m)	qarzadār
to lend (money)	कर्ज़ देना	karz dena
to borrow (vi, vt)	कर्ज़ लेना	karz lena
bank	बैंक (m)	baink
account	बैंक खाता (m)	baink khāta
to deposit into the account	बैंक खाते में जमा करना	baink khāte men jama karana
to withdraw (vt)	खाते से पैसे निकालना	khāte se paise nikālana
credit card	क्रेडिट कार्ड (m)	kredit kārd
cash	कैश (m pl)	kaish
check	चेक (m)	chek
to write a check	चेक लिखना	chek likhana
checkbook	चेकबुक (f)	chekabuk
wallet	बटुआ (m)	batua
change purse	बटुआ (m)	batua
safe	लॉकर (m)	lokar
heir	उत्तराधिकारी (m)	uttarādhikārī
inheritance	उत्तराधिकार (m)	uttarādhikār
fortune (wealth)	संपत्ति (f)	sampatti
lease	किराये पर देना (m)	kirāye par dena
rent (money)	किराया (m)	kirāya
to rent (sth from sb)	किराए पर लेना	kirae par lena
price	दाम (m)	dām

cost	कीमत (f)	kīmat
sum	रक़म (m)	raqam
to spend (vt)	खर्च करना	kharch karana
expenses	खर्च (m pl)	kharch
to economize (vi, vt)	बचत करना	bachat karana
economical	किफ़ायती	kifāyatī
to pay (vi, vt)	दाम चुकाना	dām chukāna
payment	भुगतान (m)	bhugatān
change (give the ~)	चिल्लर (m)	chillar
tax	टैक्स (m)	taiks
fine	जुर्माना (m)	jurmāna
to fine (vt)	जुर्माना लगाना	jurmāna lagāna

42. Post. Postal service

post office	डाकघर (m)	dākaghar
mail (letters, etc.)	डाक (m)	dāk
mailman	डाकिया (m)	dākiya
opening hours	खुलने का समय (m)	khulane ka samay
letter	पत्र (m)	patr
registered letter	रजिस्टरी पत्र (m)	rajistarī patr
postcard	पोस्ट कार्ड (m)	post kārd
telegram	तार (m)	tār
package (parcel)	पार्सल (f)	pārsal
money transfer	मनी ट्रांसफर (m)	manī trānsafar
to receive (vt)	पाना	pāna
to send (vt)	भेजना	bhejana
sending	भेज (m)	bhej
address	पता (m)	pata
ZIP code	पिन कोड (m)	pin kod
sender	भेजनेवाला (m)	bhejanevāla
receiver	पानेवाला (m)	pānevāla
name (first name)	पहला नाम (m)	pahala nām
surname (last name)	उपनाम (m)	upanām
postage rate	डाक दर (m)	dāk dar
standard (adj)	मानक	mānak
economical (adj)	किफ़ायती	kifāyatī
weight	वज़न (m)	vazan
to weigh (~ letters)	तोलना	tolana
envelope	लिफ़ाफ़ा (m)	lifāfa
postage stamp	डाक टिकट (m)	dāk tikat
to stamp an envelope	डाक टिकट लगाना	dāk tikat lagāna

43. Banking

bank	बैंक (m)	baink
branch (of bank, etc.)	शाखा (f)	shākha
bank clerk, consultant	क्लर्क (m)	klark
manager (director)	मैनेजर (m)	mainejar
bank account	बैंक खाता (m)	baink khāta
account number	खाते का नम्बर (m)	khāte ka nambar
checking account	चालू खाता (m)	chālū khāta
savings account	बचत खाता (m)	bachat khāta
to open an account	खाता खोलना	khāta kholana
to close the account	खाता बंद करना	khāta band karana
to deposit into the account	खाते में जमा करना	khāte men jama karana
to withdraw (vt)	खाते से पैसा निकालना	khāte se paisa nikālana
deposit	जमा (m)	jama
to make a deposit	जमा करना	jama karana
wire transfer	तार स्थानांतरण (m)	tār sthānāntaran
to wire, to transfer	पैसे स्थानांतरित करना	paise sthānāntarit karana
sum	रक़म (m)	raqam
How much?	कितना?	kitana?
signature	हस्ताक्षर (f)	hastākshar
to sign (vt)	हस्ताक्षर करना	hastākshar karana
credit card	क्रेडिट कार्ड (m)	kredit kārd
code (PIN code)	पिन कोड (m)	pin kod
credit card number	क्रेडिट कार्ड संख्या (f)	kredit kārd sankhya
ATM	एटीएम (m)	etīem
check	चेक (m)	chek
to write a check	चेक लिखना	chek likhana
checkbook	चेकबुक (f)	chekabuk
loan (bank ~)	उधार (m)	uthār
to apply for a loan	उधार के लिए आवेदन करना	udhār ke lie āvedan karana
to get a loan	उधार लेना	uthār lena
to give a loan	उधार देना	uthār dena
guarantee	गारन्टी (f)	gārantī

44. Telephone. Phone conversation

telephone	फ़ोन (m)	fon
cell phone	मोबाइल फ़ोन (m)	mobail fon

answering machine	जवाबी मशीन (f)	javābī mashīn
to call (by phone)	फ़ोन करना	fon karana
phone call	कॉल (m)	kol

to dial a number	नम्बर लगाना	nambar lagāna
Hello!	हेलो!	helo!
to ask (vt)	पूछना	pūchhana
to answer (vi, vt)	जवाब देना	javāb dena

to hear (vt)	सुनना	sunana
well (adv)	ठीक	thīk
not well (adv)	ठीक नहीं	thīk nahin
noises (interference)	आवाज़ें (f)	āvāzen

receiver	रिसीवर (m)	risīvar
to pick up (~ the phone)	फ़ोन उठाना	fon uthāna
to hang up (~ the phone)	फ़ोन रखना	fon rakhana

busy (engaged)	बिज़ी	bizī
to ring (ab. phone)	फ़ोन बजना	fon bajana
telephone book	टेलीफ़ोन बुक (m)	telīfon buk
local (adj)	लोकल	lokal
long distance (~ call)	लंबी दूरी की कॉल	lambī dūrī kī kol
international (adj)	अंतर्राष्ट्रीय	antarrāshtrīy

45. Cell phone

cell phone	मोबाइल फ़ोन (m)	mobail fon
display	डिस्प्ले (m)	disple
button	बटन (m)	batan
SIM card	सिम कार्ड (m)	sim kārd

battery	बैटरी (f)	baitarī
to be dead (battery)	बैटरी डेड हो जाना	baitarī ded ho jāna
charger	चार्जर (m)	chārjar

| menu | मीनू (m) | mīnū |
| settings | सेटिंग्स (f) | setings |

| tune (melody) | कॉलर ट्यून (m) | kolar tyūn |
| to select (vt) | चुनना | chunana |

| calculator | कैल्कुलैटर (m) | kailkulaitar |
| voice mail | वॉयस मेल (f) | voyas mel |

| alarm clock | अलार्म घड़ी (f) | alārm gharī |
| contacts | संपर्क (m) | sampark |

| SMS (text message) | एसएमएस (m) | esemes |
| subscriber | सदस्य (m) | sadasy |

46. Stationery

ballpoint pen	बॉल पेन (m)	bol pen
fountain pen	फाउन्टेन पेन (m)	faunten pen
pencil	पेंसिल (f)	pensil
highlighter	हाइलाइटर (m)	hailaitar
felt-tip pen	फ़ेल्ट टिप पेन (m)	felt tip pen
notepad	नोटबुक (m)	notabuk
agenda (diary)	डायरी (f)	dāyarī
ruler	स्केल (m)	skel
calculator	कैल्कुलेटर (m)	kailkuletar
eraser	रबड़ (f)	rabar
thumbtack	थंबटैक (m)	thanrbataik
paper clip	पेपर क्लिप (m)	pepar klip
glue	गोंद (f)	gond
stapler	स्टेप्लर (m)	steplar
hole punch	होल पंचर (m)	hol panchar
pencil sharpener	शार्पनर (m)	shārpanar

47. Foreign languages

language	भाषा (f)	bhāsha
foreign language	विदेशी भाषा (f)	videshī bhāsha
to study (vt)	पढ़ना	parhana
to learn (language, etc.)	सीखना	sīkhana
to read (vi, vt)	पढ़ना	parhana
to speak (vi, vt)	बोलना	bolana
to understand (vt)	समझना	samajhana
to write (vt)	लिखना	likhana
fast (adv)	तेज़	tez
slowly (adv)	धीरे	dhīre
fluently (adv)	धड़ल्ले से	dharalle se
rules	नियम (m pl)	niyam
grammar	व्याकरण (m)	vyākaran
vocabulary	शब्दावली (f)	shabdāvalī
phonetics	स्वरविज्ञान (m)	svaravigyān
textbook	पाठ्यपुस्तक (f)	pāthyapustak
dictionary	शब्दकोश (m)	shabdakosh
teach-yourself book	स्वयंशिक्षक पुस्तक (m)	svayanshikshak pustak
phrasebook	वार्तालाप-पुस्तिका (f)	vārttālāp-pustika
cassette, tape	कैसेट (f)	kaiset

videotape	वीडियो कैसेट (m)	vīdiyo kaiset
CD, compact disc	सीडी (m)	sīdī
DVD	डीवीडी (m)	dīvīdī
alphabet	वर्णमाला (f)	varnamāla
to spell (vt)	हिज्जे करना	hijje karana
pronunciation	उच्चारण (m)	uchchāran
accent	लहज़ा (m)	lahaza
with an accent	लहज़े के साथ	lahaze ke sāth
without an accent	बिना लहज़े	bina lahaze
word	शब्द (m)	shabd
meaning	मतलब (m)	matalab
course (e.g., a French ~)	पाठ्यक्रम (m)	pāthyakram
to sign up	सदस्य बनना	sadasy banana
teacher	शिक्षक (m)	shikshak
translation (process)	तर्जुमा (m)	tarjuma
translation (text, etc.)	अनुवाद (m)	anuvād
translator	अनुवादक (m)	anuvādak
interpreter	दुभाषिया (m)	dubhāshiya
polyglot	बहुभाषी (m)	bahubhāshī
memory	स्मृति (f)	smrti

MEALS. RESTAURANT

T&P Books Publishing

48. Table setting

spoon	चम्मच (m)	chammach
knife	छुरी (f)	chhurī
fork	काँटा (m)	kānta

cup (e.g., coffee ~)	प्याला (m)	pyāla
plate (dinner ~)	तश्तरी (f)	tashtarī
saucer	सॉसर (m)	sosar
napkin (on table)	नैपकीन (m)	naipakīn
toothpick	टूथपिक (m)	tūthapik

49. Restaurant

restaurant	रेस्टराँ (m)	restarān
coffee house	कॉफ़ी हाउस (m)	kofī haus
pub, bar	बार (m)	bār
tearoom	चायख़ाना (m)	chāyakhāna

waiter	बैरा (m)	baira
waitress	बैरी (f)	bairī
bartender	बारमैन (m)	bāramain
menu	मेनू (m)	menū
wine list	वाइन सूची (f)	vain sūchī
to book a table	मेज़ बुक करना	mez buk karana

course, dish	पकवान (m)	pakavān
to order (meal)	आर्डर देना	ārdar dena
to make an order	आर्डर देना	ārdar dena
aperitif	एपेरेतीफ़ (m)	eperetīf
appetizer	एपेटाइज़र (m)	epetaizar
dessert	मीठा (m)	mītha

check	बिल (m)	bil
to pay the check	बील का भुगतान करना	bīl ka bhugatān karana
to give change	खुले पैसे देना	khule paise dena
tip	टिप (f)	tip

50. Meals

| food | खाना (m) | khāna |
| to eat (vi, vt) | खाना खाना | khāna khāna |

breakfast	नाश्ता (m)	nāshta
to have breakfast	नाश्ता करना	nāshta karana
lunch	दोपहर का भोजन (m)	dopahar ka bhojan
to have lunch	दोपहर का भोजन करना	dopahar ka bhojan karana
dinner	रात्रिभोज (m)	rātribhoj
to have dinner	रात्रिभोज करना	rātribhoj karana
appetite	भूख (f)	bhūkh
Enjoy your meal!	अपने भोजन का आनंद उठाएं!	apane bhojan ka ānand uthaen!
to open (~ a bottle)	खोलना	kholana
to spill (liquid)	गिराना	girāna
to spill out (vi)	गिराना	girāna
to boil (vi)	उबालना	ubālana
to boil (vt)	उबालना	ubālana
boiled (~ water)	उबला हुआ	ubala hua
to chill, cool down (vt)	ठंडा करना	thanda karana
to chill (vi)	ठंडा करना	thanda karana
taste, flavor	स्वाद (m)	svād
aftertaste	स्वाद (m)	svād
to slim down (lose weight)	वज़न घटाना	vazan ghatāna
diet	डाइट (m)	dait
vitamin	विटामिन (m)	vitāmin
calorie	कैलोरी (f)	kailorī
vegetarian (n)	शाकाहारी (m)	shākāhārī
vegetarian (adj)	शाकाहारी	shākāhārī
fats (nutrient)	वसा (m pl)	vasa
proteins	प्रोटीन (m pl)	protīn
carbohydrates	कार्बोहाइड्रेट (m)	kārbohaidret
slice (of lemon, ham)	टुकड़ा (m)	tukara
piece (of cake, pie)	टुकड़ा (m)	tukara
crumb (of bread, cake, etc.)	टुकड़ा (m)	tukara

51. Cooked dishes

course, dish	पकवान (m)	pakavān
cuisine	व्यंजन (m)	vyanjan
recipe	रैसीपी (f)	raisīpī
portion	भाग (m)	bhāg
salad	सलाद (m)	salād
soup	सूप (m)	sūp
clear soup (broth)	यख़नी (f)	yakhanī
sandwich (bread)	सैन्डविच (m)	saindavich

fried eggs	आमलेट (m)	āmalet
hamburger (beefburger)	हैमबर्गर (m)	haimabargar
beefsteak	बीफ़स्टीक (m)	bīfastīk

side dish	साइड डिश (f)	said dish
spaghetti	स्पेचेटी (f)	speghetī
mashed potatoes	आलू भरता (f)	ālū bharata
pizza	पीट्ज़ा (f)	pītza
porridge (oatmeal, etc.)	दलिया (f)	daliya
omelet	आमलेट (m)	āmalet

boiled (e.g., ~ beef)	उबला	ubala
smoked (adj)	धुएँ में पकाया हुआ	dhuen men pakāya hua
fried (adj)	भुना	bhuna
dried (adj)	सूखा	sūkha
frozen (adj)	फ़्रोज़न	frozan
pickled (adj)	अचार	achār

sweet (sugary)	मीठा	mītha
salty (adj)	नमकीन	namakīn
cold (adj)	ठंडा	thanda
hot (adj)	गरम	garam
bitter (adj)	कड़वा	karava
tasty (adj)	स्वादिष्ट	svādisht

to cook in boiling water	उबलते पानी में पकाना	ubalate pānī men pakāna
to cook (dinner)	खाना बनाना	khāna banāna
to fry (vt)	भूनना	bhūnana
to heat up (food)	गरम करना	garam karana

to salt (vt)	नमक डालना	namak dālana
to pepper (vt)	मिर्च डालना	mirch dālana
to grate (vt)	कद्दूकश करना	kaddūkash karana
peel (n)	छिलका (f)	chhilaka
to peel (vt)	छिलका निकलना	chhilaka nikalana

52. Food

meat	गोश्त (m)	gosht
chicken	चीकन (m)	chīkan
Rock Cornish hen (poussin)	रॉक कोर्निश मुर्गी (f)	rok kornish murgī
duck	बत्तख़ (f)	battakh
goose	हंस (m)	hans
game	शिकार के पशुपक्षी (f)	shikār ke pashupakshī
turkey	टर्की (m)	tarkī

pork	सुअर का गोश्त (m)	suar ka gosht
veal	बछड़े का गोश्त (m)	bachhare ka gosht
lamb	भेड़ का गोश्त (m)	bher ka gosht

| beef | गाय का गोश्त (m) | gāy ka gosht |
| rabbit | खरगोश (m) | kharagosh |

sausage (bologna, pepperoni, etc.)	सॉसेज (f)	sosej
vienna sausage (frankfurter)	वियना सॉसेज (m)	viyana sosej
bacon	बेकन (m)	bekan
ham	हैम (m)	haim
gammon	सुअर की जांघ (f)	suar kī jāngh

pâté	पिसा हुआ गोश्त (m)	pisa hua gosht
liver	जिगर (f)	jigar
hamburger (ground beef)	कीमा (m)	kīma
tongue	जीभ (m)	jībh

egg	अंडा (m)	anda
eggs	अंडे (m pl)	ande
egg white	अंडे की सफ़ेदी (m)	ande kī safedī
egg yolk	अंडे की ज़र्दी (m)	ande kī zardī

fish	मछली (f)	machhalī
seafood	समुद्री खाना (m)	samudrī khāna
caviar	मछली के अंडे (m)	machhalī ke ande

crab	केकड़ा (m)	kekara
shrimp	चिंगड़ा (m)	chingara
oyster	सीप (m)	sīp
spiny lobster	लोबस्टर (m)	lobastar
octopus	ओक्टोपस (m)	oktopas
squid	स्कीड (m)	skīd

sturgeon	स्टर्जन (f)	starjan
salmon	सालमन (m)	sālaman
halibut	हैलिबट (f)	hailibat

cod	कॉड (f)	kod
mackerel	माक्रैल (f)	mākrail
tuna	टूना (f)	tūna
eel	बाम मछली (f)	bām machhalī

trout	ट्राउट मछली (f)	traut machhalī
sardine	सार्डीन (f)	sārdīn
pike	पाइक (f)	paik
herring	हेरिंग मछली (f)	hering machhalī

bread	ब्रेड (f)	bred
cheese	पनीर (m)	panīr
sugar	चीनी (f)	chīnī
salt	नमक (m)	namak
rice	चावल (m)	chāval
pasta (macaroni)	पास्ता (m)	pāsta

noodles	नूडल्स (m)	nūdals
butter	मक्खन (m)	makkhan
vegetable oil	तेल (m)	tel
sunflower oil	सूरजमुखी तेल (m)	sūrajamukhī tel
margarine	नकली मक्खन (m)	nakalī makkhan
olives	जैतून (m)	jaitūn
olive oil	जैतून का तेल (m)	jaitūn ka tel
milk	दूध (m)	dūdh
condensed milk	रबड़ी (f)	rabaṛī
yogurt	दही (m)	dahī
sour cream	खट्टी क्रीम (f)	khattī krīm
cream (of milk)	मलाई (f pl)	malaī
mayonnaise	मेयोनेज़ (m)	meyonez
buttercream	क्रीम (m)	krīm
cereal grains (wheat, etc.)	अनाज के दाने (m)	anāj ke dāne
flour	आटा (m)	āta
canned food	डिब्बाबन्ड खाना (m)	dibbāband khāna
cornflakes	कॉर्नफ्लेक्स (m)	kornafleks
honey	शहद (m)	shahad
jam	जैम (m)	jaim
chewing gum	चूइन्ग गम (m)	chūing gam

53. Drinks

water	पानी (m)	pānī
drinking water	पीने का पानी (f)	pīne ka pānī
mineral water	मिनरल वॉटर (m)	minaral votar
still (adj)	स्टिल वॉटर	stil votar
carbonated (adj)	काबोनेटेड	kārboneted
sparkling (adj)	स्पार्किलंग	spārkaling
ice	बर्फ़ (m)	barf
with ice	बर्फ़ के साथ	barf ke sāth
non-alcoholic (adj)	शराब रहित	sharāb rahit
soft drink	कोल्ड ड्रिंक (f)	kold drink
refreshing drink	शीतलक ड्रिंक (f)	shītalak drink
lemonade	लेमोनेड (m)	lemoned
liquors	शराब (m pl)	sharāb
wine	वाइन (f)	vain
white wine	सफ़ेद वाइन (f)	safed vain
red wine	लाल वाइन (f)	lāl vain
liqueur	लिकर (m)	likar
champagne	शैम्पेन (f)	shaimpen

vermouth	वर्मीठथ (f)	varmauth
whiskey	विस्की (f)	viskī
vodka	वोडका (m)	vodaka
gin	जिन (f)	jin
cognac	कोन्याक (m)	konyāk
rum	रम (m)	ram
coffee	कॉफ़ी (f)	kofī
black coffee	काली कॉफ़ी (f)	kālī kofī
coffee with milk	दूध के साथ कॉफ़ी (f)	dūdh ke sāth kofī
cappuccino	कैपूचिनो (f)	kaipūchino
instant coffee	इन्सटेन्ट-काफ़ी (f)	insatent-kāfī
milk	दूध (m)	dūdh
cocktail	कॉकटेल (m)	kokatel
milkshake	मिल्कशेक (m)	milkashek
juice	रस (m)	ras
tomato juice	टमाटर का रस (m)	tamātar ka ras
orange juice	संतरे का रस (m)	santare ka ras
freshly squeezed juice	ताज़ा रस (m)	tāza ras
beer	बियर (m)	biyar
light beer	हल्का बियर (m)	halka biyar
dark beer	डार्क बियर (m)	dārk biyar
tea	चाय (f)	chāy
black tea	काली चाय (f)	kālī chāy
green tea	हरी चाय (f)	harī chāy

54. Vegetables

vegetables	सब्ज़ियाँ (f pl)	sabziyān
greens	हरी सब्ज़ियाँ (f)	harī sabziyān
tomato	टमाटर (m)	tamātar
cucumber	खीरा (m)	khīra
carrot	गाजर (f)	gājar
potato	आलू (m)	ālū
onion	प्याज़ (m)	pyāz
garlic	लहसुन (m)	lahasun
cabbage	पत्ता गोभी (f)	patta gobhī
cauliflower	फूल गोभी (f)	fūl gobhī
Brussels sprouts	ब्रसेल्स स्प्राउट्स (m)	brasels sprauts
broccoli	ब्रोकोली (f)	brokolī
beetroot	चुकन्दर (m)	chukandar
eggplant	बैंगन (m)	baingan
zucchini	तुरई (f)	turī

| pumpkin | कद्दू | kaddū |
| turnip | शलजम (f) | shalajam |

parsley	अजमोद (f)	ajamod
dill	सोआ (m)	soa
lettuce	सलाद पत्ता (m)	salād patta
celery	सेलरी (m)	selarī
asparagus	एस्पैरेगस (m)	espairegas
spinach	पालक (m)	pālak

pea	मटर (m)	matar
beans	फली (f pl)	falī
corn (maize)	मकई (f)	makī
kidney bean	राजमा (f)	rājama

bell pepper	शिमला मिर्च (m)	shimala mirch
radish	मूली (f)	mūlī
artichoke	हाथीचक (m)	hāthīchak

55. Fruits. Nuts

fruit	फल (m)	fal
apple	सेब (m)	seb
pear	नाशपाती (f)	nāshapātī
lemon	नींबू (m)	nīmbū
orange	संतरा (m)	santara
strawberry (garden ~)	स्ट्रॉबेरी (f)	stroberī

mandarin	नारंगी (m)	nārangī
plum	आलूबुखारा (m)	ālūbukhāra
peach	आड़ू (m)	ārū
apricot	खूबानी (f)	khūbānī
raspberry	रसभरी (f)	rasabharī
pineapple	अनानास (m)	anānās

banana	केला (m)	kela
watermelon	तरबूज़ (m)	tarabūz
grape	अंगूर (m)	angūr
cherry	चेरी (f)	cherī
melon	खरबूज़ा (f)	kharabūza

grapefruit	ग्रेपफ्रूट (m)	grepafrūt
avocado	एवोकाडो (m)	evokādo
papaya	पपीता (f)	papīta
mango	आम (m)	ām
pomegranate	अनार (m)	anār

redcurrant	लाल किशमिश (f)	lāl kishamish
blackcurrant	काली किशमिश (f)	kālī kishamish
gooseberry	आमला (f)	āmala

bilberry	बिलबेरी (f)	bilaberī
blackberry	ब्लैकबेरी (f)	blaikaberī
raisin	किशमिश (m)	kishamish
fig	अंजीर (m)	anjīr
date	खजूर (m)	khajūr
peanut	मूँगफली (m)	mūngafalī
almond	बादाम (f)	bādām
walnut	अखरोट (m)	akharot
hazelnut	हेज़लनट (m)	hezalanat
coconut	नारियल (m)	nāriyal
pistachios	पिस्ता (m)	pista

56. Bread. Candy

bakers' confectionery (pastry)	मिठाई (f pl)	mithaī
bread	ब्रेड (f)	bred
cookies	बिस्कुट (m)	biskut
chocolate (n)	चॉकलेट (m)	chokalet
chocolate (as adj)	चॉकलेटी	chokaletī
candy (wrapped)	टॉफ़ी (f)	tofī
cake (e.g., cupcake)	पेस्ट्री (f)	pestrī
cake (e.g., birthday ~)	केक (m)	kek
pie (e.g., apple ~)	पाई (m)	paī
filling (for cake, pie)	फ़िलिंग (f)	filing
jam (whole fruit jam)	जैम (m)	jaim
marmalade	मुरब्बा (m)	murabba
waffles	वेफ़र (m pl)	vefar
ice-cream	आईस-क्रीम (f)	āīs-krīm

57. Spices

salt	नमक (m)	namak
salty (adj)	नमकीन	namakīn
to salt (vt)	नमक डालना	namak dālana
black pepper	काली मिर्च (f)	kālī mirch
red pepper (milled ~)	लाल मिर्च (m)	lāl mirch
mustard	सरसों (m)	sarason
horseradish	अरब मूली (f)	arab mūlī
condiment	मसाला (m)	masāla
spice	मसाला (m)	masāla

sauce	चटनी (f)	chatanī
vinegar	सिरका (m)	siraka
anise	सौंफ़ (f)	saumf
basil	तुलसी (f)	tulasī
cloves	लौंग (f)	laung
ginger	अदरक (m)	adarak
coriander	धनिया (m)	dhaniya
cinnamon	दालचीनी (f)	dālachīnī
sesame	तिल (m)	til
bay leaf	तेजपत्ता (m)	tejapatta
paprika	लाल शिमला मिर्च पाउडर (m)	lāl shimala mirch paudar
caraway	ज़ीरा (m)	zīra
saffron	ज़ाफ़रान (m)	zāfarān

T&P BOOKS

PERSONAL
INFORMATION. FAMILY

T&P Books Publishing

58. Personal information. Forms

name (first name)	पहला नाम (m)	pahala nām
surname (last name)	उपनाम (m)	upanām
date of birth	जन्म-दिवस (m)	janm-divas
place of birth	मातृभूमि (f)	mātrbhūmi
nationality	नागरिकता (f)	nāgarikata
place of residence	निवास स्थान (m)	nivās sthān
country	देश (m)	desh
profession (occupation)	पेशा (m)	pesha
gender, sex	लिंग (m)	ling
height	क़द (m)	qad
weight	वज़न (m)	vazan

59. Family members. Relatives

mother	माँ (f)	mān
father	पिता (m)	pita
son	बेटा (m)	beta
daughter	बेटी (f)	betī
younger daughter	छोटी बेटी (f)	chhotī betī
younger son	छोटा बेटा (m)	chhota beta
eldest daughter	बड़ी बेटी (f)	barī betī
eldest son	बड़ा बेटा (m)	bara beta
brother	भाई (m)	bhaī
sister	बहन (f)	bahan
cousin (masc.)	चचेरा भाई (m)	chachera bhaī
cousin (fem.)	चचेरी बहन (f)	chacherī bahan
mom, mommy	अम्मा (f)	amma
dad, daddy	पापा (m)	pāpa
parents	माँ-बाप (m pl)	mān-bāp
child	बच्चा (m)	bachcha
children	बच्चे (m pl)	bachche
grandmother	दादी (f)	dādī
grandfather	दादा (m)	dāda
grandson	पोता (m)	pota
granddaughter	पोती (f)	potī
grandchildren	पोते (m)	pote

uncle	चाचा (m)	chācha
aunt	चाची (f)	chāchī
nephew	भतीजा (m)	bhatīja
niece	भतीजी (f)	bhatījī

mother-in-law (wife's mother)	सास (f)	sās
father-in-law (husband's father)	ससुर (m)	sasur
son-in-law (daughter's husband)	दामाद (m)	dāmād
stepmother	सौतेली माँ (f)	sautelī mān
stepfather	सौतेले पिता (m)	sautele pita

infant	दूधमुँहा बच्चा (m)	dudhamunha bachcha
baby (infant)	शिशु (f)	shishu
little boy, kid	छोटा बच्चा (m)	chhota bachcha

wife	पत्नी (f)	patnī
husband	पति (m)	pati
spouse (husband)	पति (m)	pati
spouse (wife)	पत्नी (f)	patnī

married (masc.)	शादीशुदा	shādīshuda
married (fem.)	शादीशुदा	shādīshuda
single (unmarried)	अविवाहित	avivāhit
bachelor	कुँआरा (m)	kunāra
divorced (masc.)	तलाक़शुदा	talāqashuda
widow	विधवा (f)	vidhava
widower	विधुर (m)	vidhur

relative	रिश्तेदार (m)	rishtedār
close relative	सम्बंधी (m)	sambandhī
distant relative	दूर का रिश्तेदार (m)	dūr ka rishtedār
relatives	रिश्तेदार (m pl)	rishtedār

orphan (boy or girl)	अनाथ (m)	anāth
guardian (of a minor)	अभिभावक (m)	abhibhāvak
to adopt (a boy)	लड़का गोद लेना	laraka god lena
to adopt (a girl)	लड़की गोद लेना	larakī god lena

60. Friends. Coworkers

friend (masc.)	दोस्त (m)	dost
friend (fem.)	सहेली (f)	sahelī
friendship	दोस्ती (f)	dostī
to be friends	दोस्त होना	dost hona

buddy (masc.)	मित्र (m)	mitr
buddy (fem.)	सहेली (f)	sahelī

partner	पार्टनर (m)	pārtanar
chief (boss)	चीफ़ (m)	chīf
superior (n)	अधीक्षक (m)	adhīkshak
subordinate (n)	अधीनस्थ (m)	adhīnasth
colleague	सहकर्मी (m)	sahakarmī

acquaintance (person)	परिचित आदमी (m)	parichit ādamī
fellow traveler	सहगामी (m)	sahagāmī
classmate	सहपाठी (m)	sahapāthī

neighbor (masc.)	पड़ोसी (m)	parosī
neighbor (fem.)	पड़ोसन (f)	parosan
neighbors	पड़ोसी (m pl)	parosī

BOOKS

T&P

HUMAN BODY.
MEDICINE

T&P Books Publishing

head	सिर (m)	sir
face	चेहरा (m)	chehara
nose	नाक (f)	nāk
mouth	मुँह (m)	munh
eye	आँख (f)	ānkh
eyes	आँखें (f)	ānkhen
pupil	आँख की पुतली (f)	ānkh kī putalī
eyebrow	भौंह (f)	bhaunh
eyelash	बरौनी (f)	baraunī
eyelid	पलक (m)	palak
tongue	जीभ (m)	jībh
tooth	दाँत (f)	dānt
lips	होंठ (m)	honth
cheekbones	गाल की हड्डी (f)	gāl kī haddī
gum	मसूड़ा (m)	masūra
palate	तालु (m)	tālu
nostrils	नथने (m pl)	nathane
chin	ठोड़ी (f)	thorī
jaw	जबड़ा (m)	jabara
cheek	गाल (m)	gāl
forehead	माथा (m)	mātha
temple	कनपट्टी (f)	kanapattī
ear	कान (m)	kān
back of the head	सिर का पिछला हिस्सा (m)	sir ka pichhala hissa
neck	गरदन (m)	garadan
throat	गला (m)	gala
hair	बाल (m pl)	bāl
hairstyle	हेयरस्टाइल (m)	heyarastail
haircut	हेयरकट (m)	heyarakat
wig	नकली बाल (m)	nakalī bāl
mustache	मूँछें (f pl)	mūnchhen
beard	दाढ़ी (f)	dārhī
to have (a beard, etc.)	होना	hona
braid	चोटी (f)	chotī
sideburns	गलमुच्छा (m)	galamuchchha
red-haired (adj)	लाल बाल	lāl bāl
gray (hair)	सफ़ेद बाल	safed bāl

| bald (adj) | गंजा | ganja |
| bald patch | गंजाई (f) | ganjaī |

| ponytail | पोनी-टेल (f) | ponī-tel |
| bangs | बेंग (m) | beng |

62. Human body

| hand | हाथ (m) | hāth |
| arm | बाँह (m) | bānh |

finger	उँगली (m)	ungalī
thumb	अंगूठा (m)	angūtha
little finger	छोटी उंगली (f)	chhotī ungalī
nail	नाखून (m)	nākhūn

fist	मुट्ठी (m)	mutthī
palm	हथेली (f)	hathelī
wrist	कलाई (f)	kalaī
forearm	प्रकोष्ठ (m)	prakoshth
elbow	कोहनी (f)	kohanī
shoulder	कंधा (m)	kandha

leg	टाँग (f)	tāng
foot	पैर का तलवा (m)	pair ka talava
knee	घुटना (m)	ghutana
calf (part of leg)	पिंडली (f)	pindalī

| hip | जाँघ (f) | jāngh |
| heel | एड़ी (f) | erī |

body	शरीर (m)	sharīr
stomach	पेट (m)	pet
chest	सीना (m)	sīna
breast	स्तन (f)	stan

flank	कूल्हा (m)	kūlha
back	पीठ (f)	pīth
lower back	पीठ का निचला हिस्सा (m)	pīth ka nichala hissa
waist	कमर (f)	kamar

navel (belly button)	नाभी (f)	nābhī
buttocks	नितंब (m pl)	nitamb
bottom	नितम्ब (m)	nitamb

| beauty mark | सौंदर्य चिन्ह (f) | saundary chinh |
| birthmark (café au lait spot) | जन्म चिह्न (m) | janm chihn |

| tattoo | टैटू (m) | taitū |
| scar | घाव का निशान (m) | ghāv ka nishān |

63. Diseases

sickness	बीमारी (f)	bīmārī
to be sick	बीमार होना	bīmār hona
health	सेहत (f)	sehat
runny nose (coryza)	नज़ला (m)	nazala
tonsillitis	टॉन्सिल (m)	tonsil
cold (illness)	ज़ुकाम (f)	zukām
to catch a cold	ज़ुकाम हो जाना	zukām ho jāna
bronchitis	ब्रॉन्काइटिस (m)	bronkaitis
pneumonia	निमोनिया (f)	nimoniya
flu, influenza	फ़्लू (m)	flū
nearsighted (adj)	कमबीन	kamabīn
farsighted (adj)	कमज़ोर दूरदृष्टि	kamazor dūradrshti
strabismus (crossed eyes)	तिरछी नज़र (m)	tirachhī nazar
cross-eyed (adj)	तिरछी नज़रवाला	tirachhī nazaravāla
cataract	मोतिया बिंद (m)	motiya bind
glaucoma	काला मोतिया (m)	kāla motiya
stroke	स्ट्रोक (m)	strok
heart attack	दिल का दौरा (m)	dil ka daura
myocardial infarction	मायोकार्डियल इन्फ़ार्क्शन (m)	māyokārdiyal infārkshan
paralysis	लकवा (m)	lakava
to paralyze (vt)	लकवा मारना	laqava mārana
allergy	एलर्जी (f)	elarjī
asthma	दमा (f)	dama
diabetes	शूगर (f)	shūgar
toothache	दाँत दर्द (m)	dānt dard
caries	दाँत में कीड़ा (m)	dānt men kīra
diarrhea	दस्त (m)	dast
constipation	कब्ज़ (m)	kabz
stomach upset	पेट ख़राब (m)	pet kharāb
food poisoning	ख़राब खाने से हुई बीमारी (f)	kharāb khāne se huī bīmārī
to get food poisoning	ख़राब खाने से बीमार पड़ना	kharāb khāne se bīmār parana
arthritis	गठिया (m)	gathiya
rickets	बालवक्र (m)	bālavakr
rheumatism	आमवात (m)	āmavāt
atherosclerosis	धमनीकलाकाठिन्य (m)	dhamanīkalākāthiny
gastritis	जठर-शोथ (m)	jathar-shoth
appendicitis	उण्डुक-शोथ (m)	unduk-shoth

| cholecystitis | पित्ताशय (m) | pittāshay |
| ulcer | अल्सर (m) | alsar |

measles	मीज़ल्स (m)	mīzals
rubella (German measles)	जर्मन मीज़ल्स (m)	jarman mīzals
jaundice	पीलिया (m)	pīliya
hepatitis	हेपेटाइटिस (m)	hepetaitis

schizophrenia	शीज़ोफ्रेनीय (f)	shīzofrenīy
rabies (hydrophobia)	रेबीज़ (m)	rebīz
neurosis	न्यूरोसिस (m)	nyūrosis
concussion	आघात (m)	āghāt

cancer	कर्क रोग (m)	kark rog
sclerosis	काठिन्य (m)	kāthiny
multiple sclerosis	मल्टीपल स्क्लेरोसिस (m)	maltīpal sklerosis

alcoholism	शराबीपन (m)	sharābīpan
alcoholic (n)	शराबी (m)	sharābī
syphilis	सीफ़िलिस (m)	sīfilis
AIDS	ऐड्स (m)	aids

tumor	ट्यूमर (m)	tyūmar
malignant (adj)	घातक	ghātak
benign (adj)	अर्बुद	arbud

fever	बुखार (m)	bukhār
malaria	मलेरिया (f)	maleriya
gangrene	गैन्ग्रीन (m)	gaingrīn
seasickness	जहाज़ी मतली (f)	jahāzī matalī
epilepsy	मिरगी (f)	miragī

epidemic	महामारी (f)	mahāmārī
typhus	टाइफ़्रस (m)	taifas
tuberculosis	टीबी (m)	tībī
cholera	हैज़ा (f)	haiza
plague (bubonic ~)	प्लेग (f)	pleg

64. Symptoms. Treatments. Part 1

symptom	लक्षण (m)	lakshan
temperature	तापमान (m)	tāpamān
high temperature (fever)	बुखार (f)	bukhār
pulse	नब्ज़ (f)	nabz

dizziness (vertigo)	सिर का चक्कर (m)	sir ka chakkar
hot (adj)	गरम	garam
shivering	कंपकंपी (f)	kampakampī
pale (e.g., ~ face)	पीला	pīla
cough	खाँसी (f)	khānsī

to cough (vi)	खाँसना	khānsana
to sneeze (vi)	छींकना	chhīnkana
faint	बेहोशी (f)	behoshī
to faint (vi)	बेहोश होना	behosh hona
bruise (hématome)	नील (m)	nīl
bump (lump)	गुमड़ा (m)	gumara
to bang (bump)	चोट लगना	chot lagana
contusion (bruise)	चोट (f)	chot
to get a bruise	घाव लगना	ghāv lagana
to limp (vi)	लँगड़ाना	langarāna
dislocation	हड्डी खिसकना (f)	haddī khisakana
to dislocate (vt)	हड्डी खिसकना	haddī khisakana
fracture	हड्डी टूट जाना (f)	haddī tūt jāna
to have a fracture	हड्डी टूट जाना	haddī tūt jāna
cut (e.g., paper ~)	कट जाना (m)	kat jāna
to cut oneself	ख़ुद को काट लेना	khud ko kāt lena
bleeding	रक्त-स्राव (m)	rakt-srāv
burn (injury)	जला होना	jala hona
to get burned	जल जाना	jal jāna
to prick (vt)	चुभाना	chubhāna
to prick oneself	ख़ुद को चुभाना	khud ko chubhāna
to injure (vt)	घायल करना	ghāyal karana
injury	चोट (f)	chot
wound	घाव (m)	ghāv
trauma	चोट (f)	chot
to be delirious	बेहोशी में बड़बड़ाना	behoshī men barabadāna
to stutter (vi)	हकलाना	hakalāna
sunstroke	धूप आघात (m)	dhūp āghāt

65. Symptoms. Treatments. Part 2

pain, ache	दर्द (f)	dard
splinter (in foot, etc.)	चुभ जाना (m)	chubh jāna
sweat (perspiration)	पसीना (f)	pasīna
to sweat (perspire)	पसीना निकलना	pasīna nikalana
vomiting	वमन (m)	vaman
convulsions	दौरा (m)	daura
pregnant (adj)	गर्भवती	garbhavatī
to be born	जन्म लेना	janm lena
delivery, labor	पैदा करना (m)	paida karana
to deliver (~ a baby)	पैदा करना	paida karana
abortion	गर्भपात (m)	garbhapāt

breathing, respiration	साँस (f)	sāns
in-breath (inhalation)	साँस अंदर खींचना (f)	sāns andar khīnchana
out-breath (exhalation)	साँस बाहर छोड़ना (f)	sāns bāhar chhorana
to exhale (breathe out)	साँस बाहर छोड़ना	sāns bāhar chhorana
to inhale (vi)	साँस अंदर खींचना	sāns andar khīnchana

disabled person	अपाहिज (m)	apāhij
cripple	लूला (m)	lūla
drug addict	नशेबाज़ (m)	nashebāz

deaf (adj)	बहरा	bahara
mute (adj)	गूँगा	gūnga
deaf mute (adj)	बहरा और गूँगा	bahara aur gūnga

mad, insane (adj)	पागल	pāgal
madman	पगला (m)	pagala
(demented person)		
madwoman	पगली (f)	pagalī
to go insane	पागल हो जाना	pāgal ho jāna

gene	वंशाणु (m)	vanshānu
immunity	रोग प्रतिरोधक शक्ति (f)	rog pratirodhak shakti
hereditary (adj)	जन्मजात	janmajāt
congenital (adj)	पैदाइशी	paidaishī

virus	विषाणु (m)	vishānu
microbe	कीटाणु (m)	kītānu
bacterium	जीवाणु (m)	jīvānu
infection	संक्रमण (m)	sankraman

66. Symptoms. Treatments. Part 3

| hospital | अस्पताल (m) | aspatāl |
| patient | मरीज़ (m) | marīz |

diagnosis	रोग-निर्णय (m)	rog-nirnay
cure	इलाज (m)	ilāj
medical treatment	चिकित्सीय उपचार (m)	chikitsīy upachār
to get treatment	इलाज कराना	ilāj karāna
to treat (~ a patient)	इलाज करना	ilāj karana
to nurse (look after)	देखभाल करना	dekhabhāl karana
care (nursing ~)	देखभाल (f)	dekhabhāl

operation, surgery	ऑपरेशन (m)	opareshan
to bandage (head, limb)	पट्टी बाँधना	pattī bāndhana
bandaging	पट्टी (f)	pattī

vaccination	टीका (m)	tīka
to vaccinate (vt)	टीका लगाना	tīka lagāna
injection, shot	इंजेक्शन (m)	injekshan

to give an injection	इंजेक्शन लगाना	injekshan lagāna
amputation	अंगविच्छेद (f)	angavichchhed
to amputate (vt)	अंगविच्छेद करना	angavichchhed karana
coma	कोमा (m)	koma
to be in a coma	कोमा में चले जाना	koma men chale jāna
intensive care	गहन चिकित्सा (f)	gahan chikitsa
to recover (~ from flu)	ठीक हो जाना	thīk ho jāna
condition (patient's ~)	हालत (m)	hālat
consciousness	होश (m)	hosh
memory (faculty)	याददाश्त (f)	yādadāsht
to pull out (tooth)	दाँत निकालना	dānt nikālana
filling	भराव (m)	bharāv
to fill (a tooth)	दाँत को भरना	dānt ko bharana
hypnosis	हिपनोसिस (m)	hipanosis
to hypnotize (vt)	हिपनोटाइज़ करना	hipanotaiz karana

67. Medicine. Drugs. Accessories

medicine, drug	दवा (f)	dava
remedy	दवाई (f)	davaī
to prescribe (vt)	नुस्ख़ा लिखना	nusakha likhana
prescription	नुस्ख़ा (m)	nusakha
tablet, pill	गोली (f)	golī
ointment	मरहम (m)	maraham
ampule	एम्प्यूल (m)	empyūl
mixture	सिरप (m)	sirap
syrup	शरबत (m)	sharabat
pill	गोली (f)	golī
powder	चूरन (m)	chūran
gauze bandage	पट्टी (f)	pattī
cotton wool	रूई का गोला (m)	rūī ka gola
iodine	आयोडीन (m)	āyodīn
Band-Aid	बैंड-एड (m)	baind-ed
eyedropper	आई-ड्रॉपर (m)	āī-dropar
thermometer	थरमामीटर (m)	tharamāmītar
syringe	इंजेक्शन (m)	injekshan
wheelchair	व्हीलचेयर (f)	vhīlacheyar
crutches	बैसाखी (m pl)	baisākhī
painkiller	दर्द-निवारक (f)	dard-nivārak
laxative	जुलाब की गोली (f)	julāb kī golī
spirits (ethanol)	स्पिरिट (m)	spirit
medicinal herbs	जड़ी-बूटी (f)	jarī-būtī
herbal (~ tea)	जड़ी-बूटियों से बना	jarī-būtiyon se bana

T&P BOOKS

APARTMENT

T&P Books Publishing

68. Apartment

apartment	प्लैट (f)	flait
room	कमरा (m)	kamara
bedroom	सोने का कमरा (m)	sone ka kamara
dining room	खाने का कमरा (m)	khāne ka kamara
living room	बैठक (f)	baithak
study (home office)	घरेलू कार्यालय (m)	gharelū kāryālay
entry room	प्रवेश कक्ष (m)	pravesh kaksh
bathroom (room with a bath or shower)	स्नानघर (m)	snānaghar
half bath	शौचालय (m)	shauchālay
ceiling	छत (f)	chhat
floor	फ़र्श (m)	farsh
corner	कोना (m)	kona

69. Furniture. Interior

furniture	फ़र्निचर (m)	farnichar
table	मेज़ (f)	mez
chair	कुर्सी (f)	kursī
bed	पलंग (m)	palang
couch, sofa	सोफ़ा (m)	sofa
armchair	हत्थे वाली कुर्सी (f)	hatthe vālī kursī
bookcase	किताबों की अलमारी (f)	kitābon kī alamārī
shelf	शेल्फ़ (f)	shelf
wardrobe	कपड़ों की अलमारी (f)	kaparon kī alamārī
coat rack (wall-mounted ~)	खूँटी (f)	khūntī
coat stand	खूँटी (f)	khūntī
bureau, dresser	कपड़ों की अलमारी (f)	kaparon kī alamārī
coffee table	कॉफ़ी की मेज़ (f)	kofī kī mez
mirror	आईना (m)	āīna
carpet	कालीन (m)	kālīn
rug, small carpet	दरी (f)	darī
fireplace	चिमनी (f)	chimanī
candle	मोमबत्ती (f)	momabattī
candlestick	मोमबत्तीदान (m)	momabattīdān

drapes	परदे (m pl)	parade
wallpaper	वॉल पेपर (m)	vol pepar
blinds (jalousie)	जेलुज़ी (f pl)	jeluzī
table lamp	मेज़ का लैम्प (m)	mez ka laimp
wall lamp (sconce)	दिवार का लैम्प (m)	divār ka laimp
floor lamp	फ़र्श का लैम्प (m)	farsh ka laimp
chandelier	झूमर (m)	jhūmar
leg (of chair, table)	पाँव (m)	pānv
armrest	कुर्सी का हत्था (m)	kursī ka hattha
back (backrest)	कुर्सी की पीठ (f)	kursī kī pīth
drawer	दराज़ (m)	darāz

70. Bedding

bedclothes	बिस्तर के कपड़े (m)	bistar ke kapare
pillow	तकिया (m)	takiya
pillowcase	ग़िलाफ़ (m)	gilāf
duvet, comforter	रज़ाई (f)	razaī
sheet	चादर (f)	chādar
bedspread	चादर (f)	chādar

71. Kitchen

kitchen	रसोईघर (m)	rasoīghar
gas	गैस (m)	gais
gas stove (range)	गैस का चूल्हा (m)	gais ka chūlha
electric stove	बिजली का चूल्हा (m)	bijalī ka chūlha
oven	ओवन (m)	ovan
microwave oven	माइक्रोवेव ओवन (m)	maikrovev ovan
refrigerator	फ़्रिज (m)	frij
freezer	फ़्रीजर (m)	frījar
dishwasher	डिशवॉशर (m)	dishavoshar
meat grinder	कीमा बनाने की मशीन (f)	kīma banāne kī mashīn
juicer	जूसर (m)	jūsar
toaster	टोस्टर (m)	tostar
mixer	मिक्सर (m)	miksar
coffee machine	कॉफ़ी मशीन (f)	kofī mashīn
coffee pot	कॉफ़ी पॉट (m)	kofī pot
coffee grinder	कॉफ़ी पीसने की मशीन (f)	kofī pīsane kī mashīn
kettle	केतली (f)	ketalī
teapot	चायदानी (f)	chāyadānī
lid	ढक्कन (m)	dhakkan

tea strainer	छलनी (f)	chhalanī
spoon	चम्मच (m)	chammach
teaspoon	चम्मच (m)	chammach
soup spoon	चम्मच (m)	chammach
fork	काँटा (m)	kānta
knife	छुरी (f)	chhurī
tableware (dishes)	बरतन (m)	baratan
plate (dinner ~)	तश्तरी (f)	tashtarī
saucer	तश्तरी (f)	tashtarī
shot glass	जाम (m)	jām
glass (tumbler)	गिलास (m)	gilās
cup	प्याला (m)	pyāla
sugar bowl	चीनीदानी (f)	chīnīdānī
salt shaker	नमकदानी (m)	namakadānī
pepper shaker	मिर्चदानी (f)	mirchadānī
butter dish	मक्खनदानी (f)	makkhanadānī
stock pot (soup pot)	सॉसपैन (m)	sosapain
frying pan (skillet)	फ़्राइ पैन (f)	frai pain
ladle	डोई (f)	doī
colander	कालेन्डर (m)	kālendar
tray (serving ~)	थाली (m)	thālī
bottle	बोतल (f)	botal
jar (glass)	शीशी (f)	shīshī
can	डिब्बा (m)	dibba
bottle opener	बोतल ओपनर (m)	botal opanar
can opener	ओपनर (m)	opanar
corkscrew	पेंचकस (m)	penchakas
filter	फ़िल्टर (m)	filtar
to filter (vt)	फ़िल्टर करना	filtar karana
trash, garbage (food waste, etc.)	कूड़ा (m)	kūra
trash can (kitchen ~)	कूड़े की बाल्टी (f)	kūre kī bāltī

72. Bathroom

bathroom	स्नानघर (m)	snānaghar
water	पानी (m)	pānī
faucet	नल (m)	nal
hot water	गरम पानी (m)	garam pānī
cold water	ठंडा पानी (m)	thanda pānī
toothpaste	टूथपेस्ट (m)	tūthapest
to brush one's teeth	दाँत ब्रश करना	dānt brash karana

to shave (vi)	शेव करना	shev karana
shaving foam	शेविंग फ़ोम (m)	sheving fom
razor	रेज़र (f)	rezar

to wash (one's hands, etc.)	धोना	dhona
to take a bath	नहाना	nahāna
shower	शावर (m)	shāvar
to take a shower	शावर लेना	shāvar lena

bathtub	बाथटब (m)	bāthatab
toilet (toilet bowl)	संडास (m)	sandās
sink (washbasin)	सिंक (m)	sink

| soap | साबुन (m) | sābun |
| soap dish | साबुनदानी (f) | sābunadānī |

sponge	स्पंज (f)	spanj
shampoo	शैम्पू (m)	shaimpū
towel	तौलिया (f)	tauliya
bathrobe	चोगा (m)	choga

laundry (process)	धुलाई (f)	dhulaī
washing machine	वॉशिंग मशीन (f)	voshing mashīn
to do the laundry	कपड़े धोना	kapare dhona
laundry detergent	कपड़े धोने का पाउडर (m)	kapare dhone ka paudar

73. Household appliances

TV set	टीवी सेट (m)	tīvī set
tape recorder	टेप रिकार्डर (m)	tep rikārdar
VCR (video recorder)	वीडियो टेप रिकार्डर (m)	vīdiyo tep rikārdar
radio	रेडियो (m)	rediyo
player (CD, MP3, etc.)	प्लेयर (m)	pleyar

video projector	वीडियो प्रोजेक्टर (m)	vīdiyo projektar
home movie theater	होम थीएटर (m)	hom thīetar
DVD player	डीवीडी प्लेयर (m)	dīvīdī pleyar
amplifier	ध्वनि-विस्तारक (m)	dhvani-vistārak
video game console	वीडियो गेम कन्सोल (m)	vīdiyo gem kansol

video camera	वीडियो कैमरा (m)	vīdiyo kaimara
camera (photo)	कैमरा (m)	kaimara
digital camera	डीजिटल कैमरा (m)	dījital kaimara

vacuum cleaner	वैक्यूम क्लीनर (m)	vaikyūm klīnar
iron (e.g., steam ~)	इस्तरी (f)	istarī
ironing board	इस्तरी तख़्ता (m)	istarī takhta

| telephone | टेलीफ़ोन (m) | telīfon |
| cell phone | मोबाइल फ़ोन (m) | mobail fon |

typewriter	टाइपराइटर (m)	taiparaitar
sewing machine	सिलाई मशीन (f)	silaī mashīn
microphone	माइक्रोफ़ोन (m)	maikrofon
headphones	हैड्फ़ोन (m pl)	hairafon
remote control (TV)	रिमोट (m)	rimot
CD, compact disc	सीडी (m)	sīdī
cassette, tape	कैसेट (f)	kaiset
vinyl record	रिकार्ड (m)	rikārd

T&P BOOKS

THE EARTH. WEATHER

T&P Books Publishing

space	अंतरिक्ष (m)	antariksh
space (as adj)	अंतरिक्षीय	antarikshīy
outer space	अंतरिक्ष (m)	antariksh
universe	ब्रह्माण्ड (m)	brahmānd
galaxy	आकाशगंगा (f)	ākāshaganga
star	सितारा (m)	sitāra
constellation	नक्षत्र (m)	nakshatr
planet	ग्रह (m)	grah
satellite	उपग्रह (m)	upagrah
meteorite	उल्का पिंड (m)	ulka pind
comet	पुच्छल तारा (m)	puchchhal tāra
asteroid	ग्रहिका (f)	grahika
orbit	ग्रहपथ (m)	grahapath
to revolve (~ around the Earth)	चक्कर लगना	chakkar lagana
atmosphere	वातावरण (m)	vātāvaran
the Sun	सूरज (m)	sūraj
solar system	सौर प्रणाली (f)	saur pranālī
solar eclipse	सूर्य ग्रहण (m)	sūry grahan
the Earth	पृथ्वी (f)	prthvī
the Moon	चांद (m)	chānd
Mars	मंगल (m)	mangal
Venus	शुक्र (m)	shukr
Jupiter	बृहस्पति (m)	brhaspati
Saturn	शनि (m)	shani
Mercury	बुध (m)	budh
Uranus	अरुण (m)	arun
Neptune	वरूण (m)	varūn
Pluto	प्लूटो (m)	plūto
Milky Way	आकाश गंगा (f)	ākāsh ganga
Great Bear (Ursa Major)	सप्तर्षिमंडल (m)	saptarshimandal
North Star	ध्रुव तारा (m)	dhruv tāra
Martian	मंगल ग्रह का निवासी (m)	mangal grah ka nivāsī
extraterrestrial (n)	अन्य नक्षत्र का निवासी (m)	any nakshatr ka nivāsī

alien	अन्य नक्षत्र का निवासी (m)	any nakshatr ka nivāsī
flying saucer	उड़न तश्तरी (f)	uran tashtarī
spaceship	अंतरिक्ष विमान (m)	antariksh vimān
space station	अंतरिक्ष अड्डा (m)	antariksh adda
blast-off	चालू करना (m)	chālū karana
engine	इंजन (m)	injan
nozzle	नोज़ल (m)	nozal
fuel	ईंधन (m)	īndhan
cockpit, flight deck	केबिन (m)	kebin
antenna	एरियल (m)	eriyal
porthole	विमान गवाक्ष (m)	vimān gavāksh
solar panel	सौर पेनल (m)	saur penal
spacesuit	अंतरिक्ष पोशाक (m)	antariksh poshāk
weightlessness	भारहीनता (m)	bhārahīnata
oxygen	आक्सीजन (m)	āksījan
docking (in space)	डॉकिंग (f)	doking
to dock (vi, vt)	डॉकिंग करना	doking karana
observatory	वेधशाला (m)	vedhashāla
telescope	दूरबीन (f)	dūrabīn
to observe (vt)	देखना	dekhana
to explore (vt)	जाँचना	jānchana

75. The Earth

the Earth	पृथ्वी (f)	prthvī
the globe (the Earth)	गोला (m)	gola
planet	ग्रह (m)	grah
atmosphere	वातावरण (m)	vātāvaran
geography	भूगोल (m)	bhūgol
nature	प्रकृति (f)	prakrti
globe (table ~)	गोलक (m)	golak
map	नक्शा (m)	naksha
atlas	मानचित्रावली (f)	mānachitrāvalī
Europe	यूरोप (m)	yūrop
Asia	एशिया (f)	eshiya
Africa	अफ्रीका (m)	afrīka
Australia	ऑस्ट्रेलिया (m)	ostreliya
America	अमेरिका (f)	amerika
North America	उत्तरी अमेरिका (f)	uttarī amerika

South America	दक्षिणी अमेरिका (f)	dakshinī amerika
Antarctica	अंटार्कटिक (m)	antārkatik
the Arctic	आर्कटिक (m)	ārkatik

76. Cardinal directions

north	उत्तर (m)	uttar
to the north	उत्तर की ओर	uttar kī or
in the north	उत्तर में	uttar men
northern (adj)	उत्तरी	uttarī

south	दक्षिण (m)	dakshin
to the south	दक्षिण की ओर	dakshin kī or
in the south	दक्षिण में	dakshin men
southern (adj)	दक्षिणी	dakshinī

west	पश्चिम (m)	pashchim
to the west	पश्चिम की ओर	pashchim kī or
in the west	पश्चिम में	pashchim men
western (adj)	पश्चिमी	pashchimī

east	पूर्व (m)	pūrv
to the east	पूर्व की ओर	pūrv kī or
in the east	पूर्व में	pūrv men
eastern (adj)	पूर्वी	pūrvī

77. Sea. Ocean

sea	सागर (m)	sāgar
ocean	महासागर (m)	mahāsāgar
gulf (bay)	खाड़ी (f)	khārī
straits	जलग्रीवा (m)	jalagrīva

continent (mainland)	महाद्वीप (m)	mahādvīp
island	द्वीप (m)	dvīp
peninsula	प्रायद्वीप (m)	prāyadvīp
archipelago	द्वीप समूह (m)	dvīp samūh

bay, cove	तट-खाड़ी (f)	tat-khārī
harbor	बंदरगाह (m)	bandaragāh
lagoon	लैगून (m)	laigūn
cape	अंतरीप (m)	antarīp

atoll	एटोल (m)	etol
reef	रीफ़ (m)	rīf
coral	प्रवाल (m)	pravāl
coral reef	प्रवाल रीफ़ (m)	pravāl rīf
deep (adj)	गहरा	gahara

depth (deep water)	गहराई (f)	gaharaī
abyss	रसातल (m)	rasātal
trench (e.g., Mariana ~)	गढ्ढा (m)	garha
current (Ocean ~)	धारा (f)	dhāra
to surround (bathe)	घिरा होना	ghira hona
shore	किनारा (m)	kināra
coast	तटबंध (m)	tatabandh
flow (flood tide)	ज्वार (m)	jvār
ebb (ebb tide)	भाटा (m)	bhāta
shoal	रेती (m)	retī
bottom (~ of the sea)	तला (m)	tala
wave	तरंग (f)	tarang
crest (~ of a wave)	तरंग शिखर (f)	tarang shikhar
spume (sea foam)	झाग (m)	jhāg
hurricane	तुफ़ान (m)	tufân
tsunami	सुनामी (f)	sunāmī
calm (dead ~)	शांत (m)	shānt
quiet, calm (adj)	शांत	shānt
pole	ध्रुव (m)	dhruv
polar (adj)	ध्रुवीय	dhruvīy
latitude	अक्षांश (m)	akshānsh
longitude	देशान्तर (m)	deshāntar
parallel	समांतर-रेखा (f)	samāntar-rekha
equator	भूमध्य रेखा (f)	bhūmadhy rekha
sky	आकाश (f)	ākāsh
horizon	क्षितिज (m)	kshitij
air	हवा (f)	hava
lighthouse	प्रकाशस्तंभ (m)	prakāshastambh
to dive (vi)	गोता मारना	gota mārana
to sink (ab. boat)	डूब जाना	dūb jāna
treasures	खज़ाना (m)	khazāna

78. Seas' and Oceans' names

Atlantic Ocean	अटलांटिक महासागर (m)	atalāntik mahāsāgar
Indian Ocean	हिन्द महासागर (m)	hind mahāsāgar
Pacific Ocean	प्रशांत महासागर (m)	prashānt mahāsāgar
Arctic Ocean	उत्तरी ध्रुव महासागर (m)	uttarī dhuv mahāsāgar
Black Sea	काला सागर (m)	kāla sāgar
Red Sea	लाल सागर (m)	lāl sāgar

Yellow Sea	पीला सागर (m)	pīla sāgar
White Sea	सफ़ेद सागर (m)	safed sāgar
Caspian Sea	कैस्पियन सागर (m)	kaispiyan sāgar
Dead Sea	मृत सागर (m)	mrt sāgar
Mediterranean Sea	भूमध्य सागर (m)	bhūmadhy sāgar
Aegean Sea	ईजियन सागर (m)	ījiyan sāgar
Adriatic Sea	एड्रिएटिक सागर (m)	edrietik sāgar
Arabian Sea	अरब सागर (m)	arab sāgar
Sea of Japan	जापान सागर (m)	jāpān sāgar
Bering Sea	बेरिंग सागर (m)	bering sāgar
South China Sea	दक्षिण चीन सागर (m)	dakshin chīn sāgar
Coral Sea	कोरल सागर (m)	koral sāgar
Tasman Sea	तस्मान सागर (m)	tasmān sāgar
Caribbean Sea	करिबियन सागर (m)	karibiyan sāgar
Barents Sea	बैरेंट्स सागर (m)	bairents sāgar
Kara Sea	काड़ा सागर (m)	kāra sāgar
North Sea	उत्तर सागर (m)	uttar sāgar
Baltic Sea	बाल्टिक सागर (m)	bāltik sāgar
Norwegian Sea	नार्वे सागर (m)	nārve sāgar

79. Mountains

mountain	पहाड़ (m)	pahār
mountain range	पर्वत माला (f)	parvat māla
mountain ridge	पहाड़ों का सिलसिला (m)	pahāron ka silasila
summit, top	चोटी (f)	chotī
peak	शिखर (m)	shikhar
foot (~ of the mountain)	तलहटी (f)	talahatī
slope (mountainside)	ढलान (f)	dhalān
volcano	ज्वालामुखी (m)	jvālāmukhī
active volcano	सक्रिय ज्वालामुखी (m)	sakriy jvālāmukhī
dormant volcano	निष्क्रिय ज्वालामुखी (m)	nishkriy jvālāmukhī
eruption	विस्फोटन (m)	visfotan
crater	ज्वालामुखी का मुख (m)	jvālāmukhī ka mukh
magma	मैग्मा (m)	maigma
lava	लावा (m)	lāva
molten (~ lava)	पिघला हुआ	pighala hua
canyon	घाटी (m)	ghātī
gorge	तंग घाटी (f)	tang ghātī
crevice	दरार (m)	darār

pass, col	मार्ग (m)	mārg
plateau	पठार (m)	pathār
cliff	शिला (f)	shila
hill	टीला (m)	tīla

glacier	हिमनद (m)	himanad
waterfall	झरना (m)	jharana
geyser	उष्ण जल स्रोत (m)	ushn jal srot
lake	तालाब (m)	tālāb

plain	समतल प्रदेश (m)	samatal pradesh
landscape	परिदृश्य (m)	paridrshy
echo	गूँज (f)	gūnj

alpinist	पर्वतारोही (m)	parvatārohī
rock climber	पर्वतारोही (m)	parvatārohī
to conquer (in climbing)	चोटी पर पहुँचना	chotī par pahunchana
climb (an easy ~)	चढ़ाव (m)	charhāv

80. Mountains names

The Alps	आल्पस (m)	ālpas
Mont Blanc	मोन्ट ब्लैंक (m)	mont blaink
The Pyrenees	पाइरीनीज़ (f pl)	pairīnīz

The Carpathians	कार्पाथियेन्स (m)	kārpāthiyens
The Ural Mountains	यूरल (m)	yūral
The Caucasus Mountains	कोकेशिया के पहाड़ (m)	kokeshiya ke pahār
Mount Elbrus	एल्ब्रस पर्वत (m)	elbras parvat

The Altai Mountains	अल्टाई पर्वत (m)	altaī parvat
The Tian Shan	तियान शान (m)	tiyān shān
The Pamir Mountains	पामीर पर्वत (m)	pāmīr parvat
The Himalayas	हिमालय (m)	himālay
Mount Everest	माउंट एवरेस्ट (m)	maunt everest

| The Andes | एंडीज़ (f pl) | endīz |
| Mount Kilimanjaro | किलीमन्जारो (m) | kilīmanjāro |

81. Rivers

river	नदी (f)	nadī
spring (natural source)	झरना (m)	jharana
riverbed (river channel)	नदी तल (m)	nadī tal
basin (river valley)	बेसिन (m)	besin
to flow into ...	गिरना	girana
tributary	उपनदी (f)	upanadī
bank (of river)	तट (m)	tat

current (stream)	धारा (f)	dhāra
downstream (adv)	बहाव के साथ	bahāv ke sāth
upstream (adv)	बहाव के विरुद्ध	bahāv ke virūddh
inundation	बाढ़ (f)	bārh
flooding	बाढ़ (f)	bārh
to overflow (vi)	उमड़ना	umarana
to flood (vt)	पानी से भरना	pānī se bharana
shallow (shoal)	छिछला पानी (m)	chhichhala pānī
rapids	तेज़ उतार (m)	tez utār
dam	बांध (m)	bāndh
canal	नहर (f)	nahar
reservoir (artificial lake)	जलाशय (m)	jalāshay
sluice, lock	स्लूस (m)	slūs
water body (pond, etc.)	जल स्रोत (m)	jal srot
swamp (marshland)	दलदल (f)	daladal
bog, marsh	दलदल (f)	daladal
whirlpool	भंवर (m)	bhanvar
stream (brook)	झरना (m)	jharana
drinking (ab. water)	पीने का	pīne ka
fresh (~ water)	ताज़ा	tāza
ice	बर्फ़ (m)	barf
to freeze over (ab. river, etc.)	जम जाना	jam jāna

82. Rivers' names

Seine	सीन (f)	sīn
Loire	लॉयर (f)	loyar
Thames	थेम्स (f)	thems
Rhine	राइन (f)	rain
Danube	डेन्यूब (f)	denyūb
Volga	वोल्गा (f)	volga
Don	डॉन (f)	don
Lena	लेना (f)	lena
Yellow River	ह्वांग हे (f)	hvāng he
Yangtze	यांग्त्ज़ी (f)	yāngtzī
Mekong	मेकांग (f)	mekāng
Ganges	गंगा (f)	ganga
Nile River	नील (f)	nīl
Congo River	कांगो (f)	kāngo

Okavango River	ओकावान्गो (f)	okāvāngo
Zambezi River	ज़म्बेज़ी (f)	zambezī
Limpopo River	लिम्पोपो (f)	limpopo
Mississippi River	मिसिसिपी (f)	misisipī

83. Forest

| forest, wood | जंगल (m) | jangal |
| forest (as adj) | जंगली | jangalī |

thick forest	घना जंगल (m)	ghana jangal
grove	उपवान (m)	upavān
forest clearing	खुला छोटा मैदान (m)	khula chhota maidān

| thicket | झाड़ियाँ (f pl) | jhāriyān |
| scrubland | झाड़ियों भरा मैदान (m) | jhāriyon bhara maidān |

| footpath (troddenpath) | फुटपाथ (m) | futapāth |
| gully | नाली (f) | nālī |

tree	पेड़ (m)	per
leaf	पत्ता (m)	patta
leaves (foliage)	पत्तियां (f)	pattiyān

fall of leaves	पतझड़ (m)	patajhar
to fall (ab. leaves)	गिरना	girana
top (of the tree)	शिखर (m)	shikhar

branch	टहनी (f)	tahanī
bough	शाखा (f)	shākha
bud (on shrub, tree)	कलिका (f)	kalika
needle (of pine tree)	सुई (f)	suī
pine cone	शंकुफल (m)	shankufal

hollow (in a tree)	खोखला (m)	khokhala
nest	घोंसला (m)	ghonsala
burrow (animal hole)	बिल (m)	bil

trunk	तना (m)	tana
root	जड़ (f)	jar
bark	छाल (f)	chhāl
moss	काई (f)	kaī

| to uproot (remove trees or tree stumps) | उखाड़ना | ukhārana |

to chop down	काटना	kātana
to deforest (vt)	जंगल काटना	jangal kātana
tree stump	ठूंठ (m)	thūnth
campfire	अलाव (m)	alāv
forest fire	जंगल की आग (f)	jangal kī āg

to extinguish (vt)	आग बुझाना	āg bujhāna
forest ranger	वनरक्षक (m)	vanarakshak
protection	रक्षा (f)	raksha
to protect (~ nature)	रक्षा करना	raksha karana
poacher	चोर शिकारी (m)	chor shikārī
steel trap	फंदा (m)	fanda
to gather, to pick (vt)	बटोरना	batorana
to lose one's way	रास्ता भूलना	rāsta bhūlana

84. Natural resources

natural resources	प्राकृतिक संसाधन (m pl)	prākrtik sansādhan
minerals	खनिज पदार्थ (m pl)	khanij padārth
deposits	तह (f pl)	tah
field (e.g., oilfield)	क्षेत्र (m)	kshetr
to mine (extract)	खोदना	khodana
mining (extraction)	खनिकर्म (m)	khanikarm
ore	अयस्क (m)	ayask
mine (e.g., for coal)	खान (f)	khān
shaft (mine ~)	शैफ़ट (m)	shaifat
miner	खनिक (m)	khanik
gas (natural ~)	गैस (m)	gais
gas pipeline	गैस पाइप लाइन (m)	gais paip lain
oil (petroleum)	पेट्रोल (m)	petrol
oil pipeline	तेल पाइप लाइन (m)	tel paip lain
oil well	तेल का कुँआ (m)	tel ka kuna
derrick (tower)	डेरिक (m)	derik
tanker	टैंकर (m)	tainkar
sand	रेत (m)	ret
limestone	चूना पत्थर (m)	chūna patthar
gravel	बजरी (f)	bajarī
peat	पीट (m)	pīt
clay	मिट्टी (f)	mittī
coal	कोयला (m)	koyala
iron (ore)	लोहा (m)	loha
gold	सोना (m)	sona
silver	चाँदी (f)	chāndī
nickel	गिलट (m)	gilat
copper	ताँबा (m)	tānba
zinc	जस्ता (m)	jasta
manganese	अयस (m)	ayas
mercury	पारा (f)	pāra
lead	सीसा (f)	sīsa

mineral	खनिज (m)	khanij
crystal	क्रिस्टल (m)	kristal
marble	संगमरमर (m)	sangamaramar
uranium	यूरेनियम (m)	yūreniyam

85. Weather

weather	मौसम (m)	mausam
weather forecast	मौसम का पूर्वानुमान (m)	mausam ka pūrvānumān
temperature	तापमान (m)	tāpamān
thermometer	थर्मामीटर (m)	tharmāmītar
barometer	बैरोमीटर (m)	bairomītar
humidity	नमी (f)	namī
heat (extreme ~)	गरमी (f)	garamī
hot (torrid)	गरम	garam
it's hot	गरमी है	garamī hai
it's warm	गरम है	garam hai
warm (moderately hot)	गरम	garam
it's cold	ठंडक है	thandak hai
cold (adj)	ठंडा	thanda
sun	सूरज (m)	sūraj
to shine (vi)	चमकना	chamakana
sunny (day)	धूपदार	dhūpadār
to come up (vi)	उगना	ugana
to set (vi)	डूबना	dūbana
cloud	बादल (m)	bādal
cloudy (adj)	मेघाच्छादित	meghāchchhādit
rain cloud	घना बादल (m)	ghana bādal
somber (gloomy)	बदली	badalī
rain	बारिश (f)	bārish
it's raining	बारिश हो रही है	bārish ho rahī hai
rainy (~ day, weather)	बरसाती	barasātī
to drizzle (vi)	बूंदाबांदी होना	būndābāndī hona
pouring rain	मूसलधार बारिश (f)	mūsaladhār bārish
downpour	मूसलधार बारिश (f)	mūsaladhār bārish
heavy (e.g., ~ rain)	भारी	bhārī
puddle	पोखर (m)	pokhar
to get wet (in rain)	भीगना	bhīgana
fog (mist)	कुहरा (m)	kuhara
foggy	कुहरेदार	kuharedār
snow	बर्फ़ (f)	barf
it's snowing	बर्फ़ पड़ रही है	barf par rahī hai

86. Severe weather. Natural disasters

thunderstorm	गरजवाला तुफान (m)	garajavāla tufān
lightning (~ strike)	बिजली (m)	bijalī
to flash (vi)	चमकना	chamakana
thunder	गरज (m)	garaj
to thunder (vi)	बादल गरजना	bādal garajana
it's thundering	बादल गरज रहा है	bādal garaj raha hai
hail	ओला (m)	ola
it's hailing	ओले पड़ रहे हैं	ole par rahe hain
to flood (vt)	बाढ़ आ जाना	bārh ā jāna
flood, inundation	बाढ़ (f)	bārh
earthquake	भूकंप (m)	bhūkamp
tremor, quake	झटका (m)	jhataka
epicenter	अधिकेंद्र (m)	adhikendr
eruption	उद्गार (m)	udgār
lava	लावा (m)	lāva
twister	बवंडर (m)	bavandar
tornado	टोर्नेडो (m)	tornedo
typhoon	रतूफ़ान (m)	ratūfān
hurricane	समुद्री तूफ़ान (m)	samudrī tūfān
storm	तुफ़ान (m)	tufān
tsunami	सुनामी (f)	sunāmī
cyclone	चक्रवात (m)	chakravāt
bad weather	ख़राब मौसम (m)	kharāb mausam
fire (accident)	आग (f)	āg
disaster	प्रलय (m)	pralay
meteorite	उल्का पिंड (m)	ulka pind
avalanche	हिमस्खलन (m)	himaskhalan
snowslide	हिमस्खलन (m)	himaskhalan
blizzard	बर्फ़ का तुफ़ान (m)	barf ka tufān
snowstorm	बर्फ़िला तुफ़ान (m)	barfila tufān

BOOKS

FAUNA

T&P Books Publishing

87. Mammals. Predators

predator	परभक्षी (m)	parabhakshī
tiger	बाघ (m)	bāgh
lion	शेर (m)	sher
wolf	भेड़िया (m)	bheriya
fox	लोमड़ी (f)	lomri
jaguar	जागुआर (m)	jāguār
leopard	तेंदुआ (m)	tendua
cheetah	चीता (m)	chīta
black panther	काला तेंदुआ (m)	kāla tendua
puma	पहाड़ी बिलाव (m)	pahādī bilāv
snow leopard	हिम तेंदुआ (m)	him tendua
lynx	वन बिलाव (m)	van bilāv
coyote	कोयोट (m)	koyot
jackal	गीदड़ (m)	gīdar
hyena	लकड़बग्घा (m)	lakarabaggha

88. Wild animals

animal	जानवर (m)	jānavar
beast (animal)	जानवर (m)	jānavar
squirrel	गिलहरी (f)	gilaharī
hedgehog	कांटा-चूहा (m)	kānta-chūha
hare	खरगोश (m)	kharagosh
rabbit	खरगोश (m)	kharagosh
badger	बिज्जू (m)	bijjū
raccoon	रैकून (m)	raikūn
hamster	हैम्स्टर (m)	haimstar
marmot	मारमोट (m)	māramot
mole	छछूंदर (m)	chhachhūndar
mouse	चूहा (m)	chūha
rat	घूस (m)	ghūs
bat	चमगादड़ (m)	chamagādar
ermine	नेवला (m)	nevala
sable	सेबल (m)	sebal
marten	मारटेन (m)	māraten

weasel	नेवला (m)	nevala
mink	मिंक (m)	mink
beaver	ऊदबिलाव (m)	ūdabilāv
otter	ऊदबिलाव (m)	ūdabilāv
horse	घोड़ा (m)	ghora
moose	मूस (m)	mūs
deer	हिरण (m)	hiran
camel	ऊंट (m)	ūnt
bison	बाइसन (m)	baisan
aurochs	जंगली बैल (m)	jangalī bail
buffalo	भैंस (m)	bhains
zebra	ज़ेबरा (m)	zebara
antelope	मृग (f)	mrg
roe deer	मृगनी (f)	mrgnī
fallow deer	चीतल (m)	chītal
chamois	शैमी (f)	shaimī
wild boar	जंगली सुआर (m)	jangalī suār
whale	हेल (f)	hvel
seal	सील (m)	sīl
walrus	वॉलरस (m)	volaras
fur seal	फर सील (f)	far sīl
dolphin	डॉलफ़िन (f)	dolafin
bear	रीछ (m)	rīchh
polar bear	सफ़ेद रीछ (m)	safed rīchh
panda	पांडा (m)	pānda
monkey	बंदर (m)	bandar
chimpanzee	वनमानुष (m)	vanamānush
orangutan	वनमानुष (m)	vanamānush
gorilla	गोरिला (m)	gorila
macaque	अफ़्रीकन लंगूर (m)	afrikan langūr
gibbon	गिब्बन (m)	gibban
elephant	हाथी (m)	hāthī
rhinoceros	गैंडा (m)	gainda
giraffe	जिराफ़ (m)	jirāf
hippopotamus	दरियाई घोड़ा (m)	dariyaī ghora
kangaroo	कंगारू (m)	kangārū
koala (bear)	कोआला (m)	koāla
mongoose	नेवला (m)	nevala
chinchilla	चिनचीला (f)	chinachīla
skunk	स्कंक (m)	skank
porcupine	शल्यक (f)	shalyak

89. Domestic animals

cat	बिल्ली (f)	billī
tomcat	बिल्ला (m)	billa
dog	कुत्ता (m)	kutta

horse	घोड़ा (m)	ghora
stallion (male horse)	घोड़ा (m)	ghora
mare	घोड़ी (f)	ghorī

cow	गाय (f)	gāy
bull	बैल (m)	bail
ox	बैल (m)	bail

sheep (ewe)	भेड़ (f)	bher
ram	भेड़ा (m)	bhera
goat	बकरी (f)	bakarī
billy goat, he-goat	बकरा (m)	bakara

| donkey | गधा (m) | gadha |
| mule | खच्चर (m) | khachchar |

pig, hog	सुअर (m)	suar
piglet	घेंटा (m)	ghenta
rabbit	खरगोश (m)	kharagosh

| hen (chicken) | मुर्गी (f) | murgī |
| rooster | मुर्गा (m) | murga |

duck	बत्तख़ (f)	battakh
drake	नर बत्तख़ (m)	nar battakh
goose	हंस (m)	hans

| tom turkey, gobbler | नर टर्की (m) | nar tarkī |
| turkey (hen) | टर्की (f) | tarkī |

domestic animals	घरेलू पशु (m pl)	gharelū pashu
tame (e.g., ~ hamster)	पालतू	pālatū
to tame (vt)	पालतू बनाना	pālatū banāna
to breed (vt)	पालना	pālana

farm	खेत (m)	khet
poultry	मुर्गी पालन (f)	murgī pālan
cattle	मवेशी (m)	maveshī
herd (cattle)	पशु समूह (m)	pashu samūh

stable	अस्तबल (m)	astabal
pigpen	सूअरखाना (m)	sūarakhāna
cowshed	गोशाला (f)	goshāla
rabbit hutch	खरगोश का दरबा (m)	kharagosh ka daraba
hen house	मुर्गीखाना (m)	murgīkhāna

90. Birds

bird	चिड़िया (f)	chiriya
pigeon	कबूतर (m)	kabūtar
sparrow	गौरैया (f)	gauraiya
tit (great tit)	टिटरी (f)	titarī
magpie	नीलकण्ठ पक्षी (f)	nīlakanth pakshī

raven	काला कौआ (m)	kāla kaua
crow	कौआ (m)	kaua
jackdaw	कौआ (m)	kaua
rook	कौआ (m)	kaua

duck	बत्तख़ (f)	battakh
goose	हंस (m)	hans
pheasant	तीतर (m)	tītar

eagle	चील (f)	chīl
hawk	बाज़ (m)	bāz
falcon	बाज़ (m)	bāz
vulture	गिद्ध (m)	giddh
condor (Andean ~)	कॉन्डोर (m)	kondor

swan	राजहंस (m)	rājahans
crane	सारस (m)	sāras
stork	लकलक (m)	lakalak

parrot	तोता (m)	tota
hummingbird	हमिंग बर्ड (f)	haming bard
peacock	मोर (m)	mor

ostrich	शुतुरमुर्ग (m)	shuturamurg
heron	बगुला (m)	bagula
flamingo	फ्लेमिन्गो (m)	flemingo
pelican	हवासिल (m)	havāsil

| nightingale | बुलबुल (m) | bulabul |
| swallow | अबाबील (f) | abābīl |

thrush	मुखव्रण (f)	mukhavran
song thrush	मुखव्रण (f)	mukhavran
blackbird	ब्लैकबर्ड (m)	blaikabard

swift	बतासी (f)	batāsī
lark	भरत (m)	bharat
quail	वर्तक (m)	varttak

woodpecker	कठफोड़ा (m)	kathafora
cuckoo	कोयल (f)	koyal
owl	उल्लू (m)	ullū
eagle owl	गरूड़ उल्लू (m)	garūr ullū

wood grouse	तीतर (m)	tītar
black grouse	काला तीतर (m)	kāla tītar
partridge	चकोर (m)	chakor
starling	तिलिया (f)	tiliya
canary	कनारी (f)	kanārī
hazel grouse	पिंगल तीतर (m)	pingal tītar
chaffinch	फ़िंच (m)	finch
bullfinch	बुलफ़िंच (m)	bulafinch
seagull	गंगा-चिल्ली (f)	ganga-chillī
albatross	अल्बात्रोस (m)	albātros
penguin	पेंगुइन (m)	penguin

91. Fish. Marine animals

bream	ब्रीम (f)	brīm
carp	कार्प (f)	kārp
perch	पर्च (f)	parch
catfish	कैटफ़िश (f)	kaitafish
pike	पाइक (f)	paik
salmon	सैल्मन (f)	sailman
sturgeon	स्टर्जन (f)	starjan
herring	हेरिंग (f)	hering
Atlantic salmon	अटलांटिक सैल्मन (f)	atalāntik sailman
mackerel	माक्रैल (f)	mākrail
flatfish	फ़्लैटफ़िश (f)	flaitafish
zander, pike perch	पाइक पर्च (f)	paik parch
cod	कॉड (f)	kod
tuna	टूना (f)	tūna
trout	ट्राउट (f)	traut
eel	सर्पमीन (f)	sarpamīn
electric ray	विद्युत शंकुश (f)	vidyut shankush
moray eel	मोरे सर्पमीन (f)	more sarpamīn
piranha	पिरान्हा (f)	pirānha
shark	शार्क (f)	shārk
dolphin	डॉलफ़िन (f)	dolafin
whale	ह्वेल (f)	hvel
crab	केकड़ा (m)	kekara
jellyfish	जेली फ़िश (f)	jelī fish
octopus	आक्टोपस (m)	āktopas
starfish	स्टार फ़िश (f)	stār fish
sea urchin	जलसाही (f)	jalasāhī

seahorse	समुद्री घोड़ा (m)	samudrī ghora
oyster	कस्तूरा (m)	kastūra
shrimp	झींगा (f)	jhīnga
lobster	लॉब्स्टर (m)	lobsatar
spiny lobster	स्पाइनी लॉब्स्टर (m)	spainī lobsatar

92. Amphibians. Reptiles

snake	सर्प (m)	sarp
venomous (snake)	विषैला	vishaila
viper	वाइपर (m)	vaipar
cobra	नाग (m)	nāg
python	अजगर (m)	ajagar
boa	अजगर (m)	ajagar
grass snake	साँप (f)	sānp
rattle snake	रैटल सर्प (m)	raital sarp
anaconda	एनाकोन्डा (f)	enākonda
lizard	छिपकली (f)	chhipakalī
iguana	इग्यूएना (m)	igyūena
monitor lizard	मॉनिटर छिपकली (f)	monitar chhipakalī
salamander	सैलामैंडर (m)	sailāmaindar
chameleon	गिरगिट (m)	giragit
scorpion	वृश्चिक (m)	vrshchik
turtle	कछुआ (m)	kachhua
frog	मेंढक (m)	mendhak
toad	भेक (m)	bhek
crocodile	मगर (m)	magar

93. Insects

insect, bug	कीट (m)	kīt
butterfly	तितली (f)	titalī
ant	चींटी (f)	chīntī
fly	मक्खी (f)	makkhī
mosquito	मच्छर (m)	machchhar
beetle	भृंग (m)	bhrng
wasp	हड्डा (m)	hadda
bee	मधुमक्खी (f)	madhumakkhī
bumblebee	भंवरा (m)	bhanvara
gadfly (botfly)	गोमक्खी (f)	gomakkhī
spider	मकड़ी (f)	makarī
spiderweb	मकड़ी का जाल (m)	makarī ka jāl

dragonfly	व्याध-पतंग (m)	vyādh-patang
grasshopper	टिड्डा (m)	tidda
moth (night butterfly)	पतंगा (m)	patanga

cockroach	तिलचट्टा (m)	tilachatta
tick	जुँआ (m)	juna
flea	पिस्सू (m)	pissū
midge	भुनगा (m)	bhunaga

locust	टिड्डी (f)	tiddī
snail	घोंघा (m)	ghongha
cricket	झींगुर (m)	jhīngur
lightning bug	जुगनू (m)	juganū
ladybug	सोनपंखी (f)	sonapankhī
cockchafer	कोकचाफ़ (m)	kokachāf

leech	जोंक (m)	jok
caterpillar	इल्ली (f)	illī
earthworm	केंचुआ (m)	kenchua
larva	कीटडिंभ (m)	kītadimbh

T&P BOOKS

FLORA

T&P Books Publishing

tree	पेड़ (m)	per
deciduous (adj)	पर्णपाती	parnapātī
coniferous (adj)	शंकुधर	shankudhar
evergreen (adj)	सदाबहार	sadābahār
apple tree	सेब वृक्ष (m)	seb vrksh
pear tree	नाश्पाती का पेड़ (m)	nāshpātī ka per
cherry tree	चेरी का पेड़ (f)	cherī ka per
plum tree	आलूबुख़ारे का पेड़ (m)	ālūbukhāre ka per
birch	सनोबर का पेड़ (m)	sanobar ka per
oak	बलूत (m)	balūt
linden tree	लिनडेन वृक्ष (m)	linaden vrksh
aspen	आस्पेन वृक्ष (m)	āspen vrksh
maple	मेपल (m)	mepal
spruce	फर का पेड़ (m)	far ka per
pine	देवदार (m)	devadār
larch	लार्च (m)	lārch
fir tree	फर (m)	far
cedar	देवदर (m)	devadar
poplar	पोप्लर वृक्ष (m)	poplar vrksh
rowan	रोवाण (m)	rovān
willow	विलो (f)	vilo
alder	आल्डर वृक्ष (m)	āldar vrksh
beech	बीच (m)	bīch
elm	एल्म वृक्ष (m)	elm vrksh
ash (tree)	एश-वृक्ष (m)	esh-vrksh
chestnut	चेस्टनट (m)	chestanat
magnolia	मैगनोलिया (f)	maiganoliya
palm tree	ताड़ का पेड़ (m)	tār ka per
cypress	सरो (m)	saro
mangrove	मैनग्रोव (m)	mainagrov
baobab	गोरक्षी (m)	gorakshī
eucalyptus	यूकेलिप्टस (m)	yūkeliptas
sequoia	सेकोइया (f)	sekoiya

95. Shrubs

bush	झाड़ी (f)	jhārī
shrub	झाड़ी (f)	jhārī
grapevine	अंगूर की बेल (f)	angūr kī bel
vineyard	अंगूर का बाग़ (m)	angūr ka bāg
raspberry bush	रास्पबेरी की झाड़ी (f)	rāspaberī kī jhārī
redcurrant bush	लाल करेंट की झाड़ी (f)	lāl karent kī jhārī
gooseberry bush	गूज़बेरी की झाड़ी (f)	gūzaberī kī jhārī
acacia	ऐकेशिय (m)	aikeshiy
barberry	बारबेरी झाड़ी (f)	bāraberī jhārī
jasmine	चमेली (f)	chamelī
juniper	जूनिपर (m)	jūnipar
rosebush	गुलाब की झाड़ी (f)	gulāb kī jhārī
dog rose	जंगली गुलाब (m)	jangalī gulāb

96. Fruits. Berries

fruit	फल (m)	fal
fruits	फल (m pl)	fal
apple	सेब (m)	seb
pear	नाश्पाती (f)	nāshpātī
plum	आलूबुखारा (m)	ālūbukhāra
strawberry (garden ~)	स्ट्रॉबेरी (f)	stroberī
cherry	चेरी (f)	cherī
grape	अंगूर (m)	angūr
raspberry	रास्पबेरी (f)	rāspaberī
blackcurrant	काली करेंट (f)	kālī karent
redcurrant	लाल करेंट (f)	lāl karent
gooseberry	गूज़बेरी (f)	gūzaberī
cranberry	क्रेनबेरी (f)	krenaberī
orange	संतरा (m)	santara
mandarin	नारंगी (f)	nārangī
pineapple	अनानास (m)	anānās
banana	केला (m)	kela
date	खजूर (m)	khajūr
lemon	नींबू (m)	nīmbū
apricot	खूबानी (f)	khūbānī
peach	आड़ू (m)	ārū
kiwi	चीकू (m)	chīkū
grapefruit	ग्रेपफ्रूट (m)	grepafrūt

berry	बेरी (f)	berī
berries	बेरियां (f pl)	beriyān
cowberry	काओबेरी (f)	kaoberī
wild strawberry	जंगली स्ट्रॉबेरी (f)	jangalī stroberī
bilberry	बिलबेरी (f)	bilaberī

97. Flowers. Plants

| flower | फूल (m) | fūl |
| bouquet (of flowers) | गुलदस्ता (m) | guladasta |

rose (flower)	गुलाब (f)	gulāb
tulip	ट्यूलिप (m)	tyūlip
carnation	गुलनार (m)	gulanār
gladiolus	ग्लेडियोलस (m)	glediyolas

cornflower	नीलकूपी (m)	nīlakūpī
harebell	ब्लूबेल (m)	blūbel
dandelion	कुकरौंधा (m)	kukaraundha
camomile	कैमोमाइल (m)	kaimomail

aloe	मुसब्बर (m)	musabbar
cactus	कैक्टस (m)	kaiktas
rubber plant, ficus	रबड़ का पौधा (m)	rabar ka paudha

lily	कुमुदिनी (f)	kumudinī
geranium	जेरेनियम (m)	jeraniyam
hyacinth	हायसिंथ (m)	hāyasinth

mimosa	मिमोसा (m)	mimosa
narcissus	नरगिस (f)	naragis
nasturtium	नस्टाशयम (m)	nastāshayam

orchid	आर्किड (m)	ārkid
peony	पियोनी (m)	piyonī
violet	वॉयलेट (m)	voyalet

pansy	पैंज़ी (m pl)	painzī
forget-me-not	फर्गैट मी नाट (m)	fargent mī nāt
daisy	गुलबहार (f)	gulabahār

poppy	खशखाश (m)	khashakhāsh
hemp	भांग (f)	bhāng
mint	पुदीना (m)	pudīna

| lily of the valley | कामुदिनी (f) | kāmudinī |
| snowdrop | सफ़ेद फूल (m) | safed fūl |

| nettle | बिच्छू बूटी (f) | bichchhū būtī |
| sorrel | सोरेल (m) | sorel |

water lily	कुमुदिनी (f)	kumudinī
fern	फ़न (m)	farn
lichen	शैवाक (m)	shaivāk

greenhouse (tropical ~)	शीशाघर (m)	shīshāghar
lawn	घास का मैदान (m)	ghās ka maidān
flowerbed	फुलवारी (f)	fulavārī

plant	पौधा (m)	paudha
grass	घास (f)	ghās
blade of grass	तिनका (m)	tinaka

leaf	पत्ती (f)	pattī
petal	पंखड़ी (f)	pankharī
stem	डंडी (f)	dandī
tuber	कंद (m)	kand

| young plant (shoot) | अंकुर (m) | ankur |
| thorn | कांटा (m) | kānta |

to blossom (vi)	खिलना	khilana
to fade, to wither	मुरझाना	murajhāna
smell (odor)	बू (m)	bū
to cut (flowers)	काटना	kātana
to pick (a flower)	तोड़ना	torana

98. Cereals, grains

grain	दाना (m)	dāna
cereal crops	अनाज की फ़सलें (m pl)	anāj kī fasalen
ear (of barley, etc.)	बाल (f)	bāl

wheat	गेहूं (m)	gehūn
rye	रई (f)	raī
oats	जई (f)	jaī
millet	बाजरा (m)	bājara
barley	जौ (m)	jau

corn	मक्का (m)	makka
rice	चावल (m)	chāval
buckwheat	मोथी (m)	mothī

pea plant	मटर (m)	matar
kidney bean	राजमा (f)	rājama
soy	सोया (m)	soya
lentil	दाल (m)	dāl
beans (pulse crops)	फली (f pl)	falī

COUNTRIES OF THE WORLD

T&P Books Publishing

Afghanistan	अफ़ग़ानिस्तान (m)	afagānistān
Albania	अल्बानिया (m)	albāniya
Argentina	अर्जेंटीना (m)	arjentīna
Armenia	आर्मीनिया (m)	ārmīniya
Australia	आस्ट्रेलिया (m)	āstreliya
Austria	ऑस्ट्रिया (m)	ostriya
Azerbaijan	आज़रबाइजान (m)	āzarabaijān
The Bahamas	बहामा (m)	bahāma
Bangladesh	बांग्लादेश (m)	bānglādesh
Belarus	बेलारूस (m)	belārūs
Belgium	बेल्जियम (m)	beljiyam
Bolivia	बोलीविया (m)	bolīviya
Bosnia and Herzegovina	बोस्निया और हर्ज़ेगोविना	bosniya aur harzegovina
Brazil	ब्राज़ील (m)	brāzīl
Bulgaria	बुल्गारिया (m)	bulgāriya
Cambodia	कम्बोडिया (m)	kambodiya
Canada	कनाडा (m)	kanāda
Chile	चिली (m)	chilī
China	चीन (m)	chīn
Colombia	कोलम्बिया (m)	kolambiya
Croatia	क्रोएशिया (m)	kroeshiya
Cuba	क्यूबा (m)	kyūba
Cyprus	साइप्रस (m)	saipras
Czech Republic	चेक गणतंत्र (m)	chek ganatantr
Denmark	डेन्मार्क (m)	denmārk
Dominican Republic	डोमिनिकन रिपब्लिक (m)	dominikan ripablik
Ecuador	इक्वेडोर (m)	ikvedor
Egypt	मिस्र (m)	misr
England	इंग्लैंड (m)	inglaind
Estonia	एस्तोनिया (m)	estoniya
Finland	फ़िनलैंड (m)	finalaind
France	फ़्रांस (m)	frāns
French Polynesia	फ्रेंच पॉलीनेशिया (m)	french polīneshiya
Georgia	जॉर्जिया (m)	jorjiya
Germany	जर्मन (m)	jarman
Ghana	घाना (m)	ghāna
Great Britain	ग्रेट ब्रिटेन (m)	gret briten
Greece	ग्रीस (m)	grīs
Haiti	हाइटी (m)	haitī
Hungary	हंगरी (m)	hangarī

100. Countries. Part 2

Iceland	आयसलैंड (m)	āyasalaind
India	भारत (m)	bhārat
Indonesia	इण्डोनेशिया (m)	indoneshiya
Iran	इरान (m)	irān
Iraq	इराक़ (m)	irāq
Ireland	आयरलैंड (m)	āyaralaind
Israel	इस्रायल (m)	isrāyal
Italy	इटली (m)	italī
Jamaica	जमैका (m)	jamaika
Japan	जापान (m)	jāpān
Jordan	जॉर्डन (m)	jordan
Kazakhstan	कज़ाकस्तान (m)	kazākastān
Kenya	केन्या (m)	kenya
Kirghizia	किर्गीज़िया (m)	kirgīziya
Kuwait	कुवैत (m)	kuvait
Laos	लाओस (m)	laos
Latvia	लाटविया (m)	lātaviya
Lebanon	लेबनान (m)	lebanān
Libya	लीबिया (m)	lībiya
Liechtenstein	लिकटेंस्टीन (m)	likatenstīn
Lithuania	लिथुआनिया (m)	lithuāniya
Luxembourg	लक्ज़मबर्ग (m)	lakzamabarg
Macedonia (Republic of ~)	मेसेडोनिया (m)	mesedoniya
Madagascar	मडागास्कार (m)	madāgāskār
Malaysia	मलेशिया (m)	maleshiya
Malta	माल्टा (m)	mālta
Mexico	मेक्सिको (m)	meksiko
Moldova, Moldavia	मोलदोवा (m)	moladova
Monaco	मोनाको (m)	monāko
Mongolia	मंगोलिया (m)	mangoliya
Montenegro	मोंटेनेग्रो (m)	montenegro
Morocco	मोरक्को (m)	morakko
Myanmar	म्यांमर (m)	myāmmar
Namibia	नामीबिया (m)	nāmībiya
Nepal	नेपाल (m)	nepāl
Netherlands	नीदरलैंड्स (m)	nīdaralainds
New Zealand	न्यू ज़ीलैंड (m)	nyū zīlaind
North Korea	उत्तर कोरिया (m)	uttar koriya
Norway	नार्वे (m)	nārve

101. Countries. Part 3

Pakistan	पाकिस्तान (m)	pākistān
Palestine	फिलिस्तीन (m)	filistīn

Panama	पनामा (m)	panāma
Paraguay	परागुआ (m)	parāgua
Peru	पेरू (m)	perū
Poland	पोलैंड (m)	polaind
Portugal	पुर्तगाल (m)	purtagāl
Romania	रोमानिया (m)	romāniya
Russia	रूस (m)	rūs

Saudi Arabia	सऊदी अरब (m)	saūdī arab
Scotland	स्कॉटलैंड (m)	skotalaind
Senegal	सेनेगाल (m)	senegāl
Serbia	सर्बिया (m)	sarbiya
Slovakia	स्लोवाकिया (m)	slovākiya
Slovenia	स्लोवेनिया (m)	sloveniya

South Africa	दक्षिण अफ़्रीका (m)	dakshin afrīka
South Korea	दक्षिण कोरिया (m)	dakshin koriya
Spain	स्पेन (m)	spen
Suriname	सूरीनाम (m)	sūrīnām
Sweden	स्वीडन (m)	svīdan
Switzerland	स्विट्ज़रलैंड (m)	svitzaralaind
Syria	सीरिया (m)	sīriya

Taiwan	ताइवान (m)	taivān
Tajikistan	ताजिकिस्तान (m)	tājikistān
Tanzania	तंज़ानिया (m)	tanzāniya
Tasmania	तास्मानिया (m)	tāsmāniya
Thailand	थाईलैंड (m)	thailaind
Tunisia	ट्यूनीसिया (m)	tyunīsiya
Turkey	तुर्की (m)	turkī
Turkmenistan	तुर्कमानिस्तान (m)	turkamānistān

Ukraine	यूक्रेन (m)	yūkren
United Arab Emirates	संयुक्त अरब अमीरात (m)	sanyukt arab amīrāt
United States of America	संयुक्त राज्य अमरीका (m)	sanyukt rājy amarīka
Uruguay	उरुग्वे (m)	urugve
Uzbekistan	उज़्बेकिस्तान (m)	uzbekistān

Vatican	वेटिकन (m)	vetikan
Venezuela	वेनेज़ुएला (m)	venezuela
Vietnam	वियतनाम (m)	viyatanām
Zanzibar	ज़ैंज़िबार (m)	zainzibār

GASTRONOMIC GLOSSARY

This section contains a lot of words and terms associated with food. This dictionary will make it easier for you to understand the menu at a restaurant and choose the right dish

T&P Books Publishing

English-Hindi gastronomic glossary

aftertaste	स्वाद (m)	svād
almond	बादाम (f)	bādām
anise	सौंफ़ (f)	saumf
aperitif	एपेरेतीफ़ (m)	eperetīf
appetite	भूख (f)	bhūkh
appetizer	एपेटाइज़र (m)	epetaizar
apple	सेब (m)	seb
apricot	खूबानी (f)	khūbānī
artichoke	हाथीचक (m)	hāthīchak
asparagus	एस्पैरेगस (m)	espairegas
Atlantic salmon	अटलांटिक सैल्मन (f)	atalāntik sailman
avocado	एवोकाडो (m)	evokādo
bacon	बेकन (m)	bekan
banana	केला (m)	kela
barley	जौ (m)	jau
bartender	बारमैन (m)	bāramain
basil	तुलसी (f)	tulasī
bay leaf	तेजपत्ता (m)	tejapatta
beans	फली (f pl)	falī
beef	गाय का गोश्त (m)	gāy ka gosht
beer	बियर (m)	biyar
beetroot	चुकन्दर (m)	chukandar
bell pepper	शिमला मिर्च (m)	shimala mirch
berries	बेरियां (f pl)	beriyān
berry	बेरी (f)	berī
bilberry	बिलबेरी (f)	bilaberī
birch bolete	बर्च बोलेट (f)	barch bolet
bitter	कड़वा	karava
black coffee	काली कॉफ़ी (f)	kālī kofī
black pepper	काली मिर्च (f)	kālī mirch
black tea	काली चाय (f)	kālī chāy
blackberry	ब्लैकबेरी (f)	blaikaberī
blackcurrant	काली किशमिश (f)	kālī kishamish
boiled	उबला	ubala
bottle opener	बोतल ओपनर (m)	botal opanar
bread	ब्रेड (f)	bred
breakfast	नाश्ता (m)	nāshta
bream	ब्रीम (f)	brīm
broccoli	ब्रोकोली (f)	brokolī
Brussels sprouts	ब्रसेल्स स्प्राउट्स (m)	brasels sprauts
buckwheat	मोथी (m)	mothī
butter	मक्खन (m)	makkhan
buttercream	क्रीम (m)	krīm
cabbage	पत्ता गोभी (f)	patta gobhī

cake	पेस्ट्री (f)	pestrī
cake	केक (m)	kek
calorie	कैलोरी (f)	kailorī
can opener	ओपनर (m)	opanar
candy	टॉफ़ी (f)	tofī
canned food	डिब्बाबन्द खाना (m)	dibbāband khāna
cappuccino	कैपूचिनो (f)	kaipūchino
caraway	ज़ीरा (m)	zīra
carbohydrates	काबोहाइड्रेट (m)	kārbohaidret
carbonated	काबोनेटेड	kārboneted
carp	कार्प (f)	kārp
carrot	गाजर (f)	gājar
catfish	कैटफ़िश (f)	kaitafish
cauliflower	फूल गोभी (f)	fūl gobhī
caviar	मछली के अंडे (m)	machhalī ke ande
celery	सेलरी (m)	selarī
cep	सफ़ेद गगन-धूलि (f)	safed gagan-dhūli
cereal crops	अनाज की फ़सलें (m pl)	anāj kī fasalen
cereal grains	अनाज के दाने (m)	anāj ke dāne
champagne	शैम्पेन (f)	shaimpen
chanterelle	शेंटरेल (f)	shentarel
check	बिल (m)	bil
cheese	पनीर (m)	panīr
chewing gum	चूइन्ग गम (m)	chūing gam
chicken	चीकन (m)	chīkan
chocolate	चॉकलेट (m)	chokalet
chocolate	चॉकलेटी	chokaletī
cinnamon	दालचीनी (f)	dālachīnī
clear soup	यख़नी (f)	yakhanī
cloves	लौंग (f)	laung
cocktail	कॉकटेल (m)	kokatel
coconut	नारियल (m)	nāriyal
cod	कॉड (f)	kod
coffee	कॉफ़ी (f)	kofī
coffee with milk	दूध के साथ कॉफ़ी (f)	dūdh ke sāth kofī
cognac	कोन्याक (m)	konyāk
cold	ठंडा	thanda
condensed milk	रबड़ी (f)	rabarī
condiment	मसाला (m)	masāla
confectionery	मिठाई (f pl)	mithaī
cookies	बिस्कुट (m)	biskut
coriander	धनिया (m)	dhaniya
corkscrew	पेंचकस (m)	penchakas
corn	मकई (f)	makī
corn	मक्का (m)	makka
cornflakes	कॉर्नफ़्लेक्स (m)	kornafleks
course, dish	पकवान (m)	pakavān
cowberry	काओबेरी (f)	kaoberī
crab	केकड़ा (m)	kekara
cranberry	क्रेनबेरी (f)	krenaberī
cream	मलाई (f pl)	malaī
crumb	टुकड़ा (m)	tukara

cucumber	खीरा (m)	khīra
cuisine	व्यंजन (m)	vyanjan
cup	प्याला (m)	pyāla
dark beer	डार्क बियर (m)	dārk biyar
date	खजूर (m)	khajūr
death cap	डेथ कैप (f)	deth kaip
dessert	मीठा (m)	mītha
diet	डाइट (m)	dait
dill	सोआ (m)	soa
dinner	रात्रिभोज (m)	rātribhoj
dried	सूखा	sūkha
drinking water	पीने का पानी (f)	pīne ka pānī
duck	बतख़ (f)	battakh
ear	बाल (f)	bāl
edible mushroom	खाने योग्य गगन-धूलि (f)	khāne yogy gagan-dhūli
eel	बाम मछली (f)	bām machhalī
egg	अंडा (m)	anda
egg white	अंडे की सफ़ेदी (m)	ande kī safedī
egg yolk	अंडे की ज़र्दी (m)	ande kī zardī
eggplant	बैंगन (m)	baingan
eggs	अंडे (m pl)	ande
Enjoy your meal!	अपने भोजन का आनंद उठाए!	apane bhojan ka ānand uthaen!
fats	वसा (m pl)	vasa
fig	अंजीर (m)	anjīr
filling	फ़िलिंग (f)	filing
fish	मछली (f)	machhalī
flatfish	फ़्लैटफ़िश (f)	flaitafish
flour	आटा (m)	āta
fly agaric	फ्लाई ऐगेरिक (f)	flaī aigerik
food	खाना (m)	khāna
fork	काँटा (m)	kānta
freshly squeezed juice	ताज़ा रस (m)	tāza ras
fried	भुना	bhuna
fried eggs	ऑमलेट (m)	āmalet
frozen	फ्रोज़न	frozan
fruit	फल (m)	fal
fruits	फल (m pl)	fal
game	शिकार के पशुपक्षी (f)	shikār ke pashupakshī
gammon	सुअर की जांघ (f)	suar kī jāngh
garlic	लहसुन (m)	lahasun
gin	जिन (f)	jin
ginger	अदरक (m)	adarak
glass	गिलास (m)	gilās
glass	वाइन गिलास (m)	vain gilās
goose	हंस (m)	hans
gooseberry	आमला (f)	āmala
grain	दाना (m)	dāna
grape	अंगूर (m)	angūr
grapefruit	ग्रेपफ्रूट (m)	grepafrūt
green tea	हरी चाय (f)	harī chāy
greens	हरी सब्ज़ियाँ (f)	harī sabziyān

halibut	हैलिबट (f)	hailibat
ham	हैम (m)	haim
hamburger	कीमा (m)	kīma
hamburger	हैमबर्गर (m)	haimabargar
hazelnut	हेज़लनट (m)	hezalanat
herring	हेरिंग मछली (f)	hering machhalī
honey	शहद (m)	shahad
horseradish	अरब मूली (f)	arab mūlī
hot	गरम	garam
ice	बर्फ़ (m)	barf
ice-cream	आईस-क्रीम (f)	āīs-krīm
instant coffee	इन्सटेन्ट-काफ़ी (f)	insatent-kāfī
jam	जैम (m)	jaim
jam	जैम (m)	jaim
juice	रस (m)	ras
kidney bean	राजमा (f)	rājama
kiwi	चीकू (m)	chīkū
knife	छुरी (f)	chhurī
lamb	भेड़ का गोश्त (m)	bher ka gosht
lemon	नींबू (m)	nīmbū
lemonade	लेमोनेड (m)	lemoned
lentil	दाल (m)	dāl
lettuce	सलाद पत्ता (m)	salād patta
light beer	हल्का बियर (m)	halka biyar
liqueur	लिकर (m)	likar
liquors	शराब (m pl)	sharāb
liver	जिगर (f)	jigar
lunch	दोपहर का भोजन (m)	dopahar ka bhojan
mackerel	माक्रैल (f)	mākrail
mandarin	नारंगी (m)	nārangī
mango	आम (m)	ām
margarine	नकली मक्खन (m)	nakalī makkhan
marmalade	मुरब्बा (m)	murabba
mashed potatoes	आलू भरता (f)	ālū bharata
mayonnaise	मेयोनेज़ (m)	meyonez
meat	गोश्त (m)	gosht
melon	खरबूज़ा (f)	kharabūza
menu	मेनू (m)	menū
milk	दूध (m)	dūdh
milkshake	मिल्कशेक (m)	milkashek
millet	बाजरा (m)	bājara
mineral water	मिनरल वॉटर (m)	minaral votar
morel	मोरेल (f)	morel
mushroom	गगन-धूलि (f)	gagan-dhūli
mustard	सरसों (m)	sarason
non-alcoholic	शराब रहित	sharāb rahit
noodles	नूडल्स (m)	nūdals
oats	जई (f)	jaī
olive oil	जैतून का तेल (m)	jaitūn ka tel
olives	जैतून (m)	jaitūn
omelet	आमलेट (m)	āmalet
onion	प्याज़ (m)	pyāz

orange	संतरा (m)	santara
orange juice	संतरे का रस (m)	santare ka ras
orange-cap boletus	नारंगी छुतरी वाली गगन-धूलि (f)	nārangī chhatarī vālī gagan-dhūli
oyster	सीप (m)	sīp
pâté	पिसा हुआ गोश्त (m)	pisa hua gosht
papaya	पपीता (f)	papīta
paprika	लाल शिमला मिर्च पाउडर (m)	lāl shimala mirch paudar
parsley	अजमोद (f)	ajamod
pasta	पास्ता (m)	pāsta
pea	मटर (m)	matar
peach	आड़ू (m)	ārū
peanut	मूँगफली (m)	mūngafalī
pear	नाशपाती (f)	nāshapātī
peel	छिलका (f)	chhilaka
perch	पर्च (f)	parch
pickled	अचार	achār
pie	पाई (m)	paī
piece	टुकड़ा (m)	tukara
pike	पाइक (f)	paik
pike perch	पाइक पर्च (f)	paik parch
pineapple	अनानास (m)	anānās
pistachios	पिस्ता (m)	pista
pizza	पीट्ज़ा (f)	pītza
plate	तश्तरी (f)	tashtarī
plum	आलूबुखारा (m)	ālūbukhāra
poisonous mushroom	ज़हरीली गगन-धूलि (f)	zaharīlī gagan-dhūli
pomegranate	अनार (m)	anār
pork	सुअर का गोश्त (m)	suar ka gosht
porridge	दलिया (f)	daliya
portion	भाग (m)	bhāg
potato	आलू (m)	ālū
proteins	प्रोटीन (m pl)	protīn
pub, bar	बार (m)	bār
pumpkin	कद्दू	kaddū
rabbit	खरगोश (m)	kharagosh
radish	मूली (f)	mūlī
raisin	किशमिश (m)	kishamish
raspberry	रसभरी (f)	rasabharī
recipe	रैसीपी (f)	raisīpī
red pepper	लाल मिर्च (m)	lāl mirch
red wine	लाल वाइन (f)	lāl vain
redcurrant	लाल किशमिश (f)	lāl kishamish
refreshing drink	शीतलक ड्रिंक (f)	shītalak drink
rice	चावल (m)	chāval
rum	रम (m)	ram
russula	रसुला (f)	rasula
rye	रई (f)	raī
saffron	ज़ाफ़रान (m)	zāfarān
salad	सलाद (m)	salād
salmon	सालमन (m)	sālaman

salt	नमक (m)	namak
salty	नमकीन	namakīn
sandwich	सैन्डविच (m)	saindavich
sardine	सार्डीन (f)	sārdīn
sauce	चटनी (f)	chatanī
saucer	सॉसर (m)	sosar
sausage	सॉसेज (f)	sosej
seafood	समुद्री खाना (m)	samudrī khāna
sesame	तिल (m)	til
shark	शार्क (f)	shārk
shrimp	चिंगड़ा (m)	chingara
side dish	साइड डिश (f)	said dish
slice	टुकड़ा (m)	tukara
smoked	धुएँ में पकाया हुआ	dhuen men pakāya hua
soft drink	कोल्ड ड्रिंक (f)	kold drink
soup	सूप (m)	sūp
soup spoon	चम्मच (m)	chammach
sour cream	खट्टी क्रीम (f)	khattī krīm
soy	सोया (m)	soya
spaghetti	स्पेचेटी (f)	speghetī
sparkling	स्पार्कलिंग	spārkaling
spice	मसाला (m)	masāla
spinach	पालक (m)	pālak
spiny lobster	लोबस्टर (m)	lobastar
spoon	चम्मच (m)	chammach
squid	स्कीड (m)	skīd
steak	बीफ़स्टीक (m)	bīfastīk
still	स्टिल वॉटर	stil votar
strawberry	स्ट्रॉबेरी (f)	stroberī
sturgeon	स्टर्जन (f)	starjan
sugar	चीनी (f)	chīnī
sunflower oil	सूरजमुखी तेल (m)	sūrajamukhī tel
sweet	मीठा	mītha
taste, flavor	स्वाद (m)	svād
tasty	स्वादिष्ट	svādisht
tea	चाय (f)	chāy
teaspoon	चम्मच (m)	chammach
tip	टिप (f)	tip
tomato	टमाटर (m)	tamātar
tomato juice	टमाटर का रस (m)	tamātar ka ras
tongue	जीभ (m)	jībh
toothpick	टूथपिक (m)	tūthapik
trout	ट्राउट मछली (f)	traut machhalī
tuna	टूना (f)	tūna
turkey	टर्की (m)	tarkī
turnip	शलजम (f)	shalajam
veal	बछड़े का गोश्त (m)	bachhare ka gosht
vegetable oil	तेल (m)	tel
vegetables	सब्ज़ियाँ (f pl)	sabziyān
vegetarian	शाकाहारी (m)	shākāhārī
vegetarian	शाकाहारी	shākāhārī
vermouth	वर्माउथ (f)	varmauth

vienna sausage	वियना सॉसेज (m)	viyana sosej
vinegar	सिरका (m)	siraka
vitamin	विटामिन (m)	vitāmin
vodka	वोडका (m)	vodaka
waffles	वेफ़र (m pl)	vefar
waiter	बैरा (m)	baira
waitress	बैरी (f)	bairī
walnut	अखरोट (m)	akharot
water	पानी (m)	pānī
watermelon	तरबूज़ (m)	tarabūz
wheat	गेहूं (m)	gehūn
whiskey	विस्की (f)	viskī
white wine	सफ़ेद वाइन (f)	safed vain
wild strawberry	जंगली स्ट्रॉबेरी (f)	jangalī stroberī
wine	वाइन (f)	vain
wine list	वाइन सूची (f)	vain sūchī
with ice	बर्फ़ के साथ	barf ke sāth
yogurt	दही (m)	dahī
zucchini	तुरई (f)	turī

Hindi-English gastronomic glossary

आईस-क्रीम (f)	āīs-krīm	ice-cream
आलू (m)	ālū	potato
आलू भरता (f)	ālū bharata	mashed potatoes
आलूबुखारा (m)	ālūbukhāra	plum
आम (m)	ām	mango
आमला (f)	āmala	gooseberry
आमलेट (m)	āmalet	fried eggs
आमलेट (m)	āmalet	omelet
आड़ू (m)	ārū	peach
आटा (m)	āta	flour
अचार	achār	pickled
अदरक (m)	adarak	ginger
अजमोद (f)	ajamod	parsley
अखरोट (m)	akharot	walnut
अनाज की फ़सलें (m pl)	anāj kī fasalen	cereal crops
अनाज के दाने (m)	anāj ke dāne	cereal grains
अनानास (m)	anānās	pineapple
अनार (m)	anār	pomegranate
अंडा (m)	anda	egg
अंडे (m pl)	ande	eggs
अंडे की सफ़ेदी (m)	ande kī safeɗī	egg white
अंडे की ज़र्दी (m)	ande kī zardī	egg yolk
अंगूर (m)	angūr	grape
अंजीर (m)	anjīr	fig
अपने भोजन का आनंद उठाएं!	apane bhojan ka ānand uthaen!	Enjoy your meal!
अरब मूली (f)	arab mūlī	horseradish
अटलांटिक सैल्मन (f)	atalāntik sailman	Atlantic salmon
बादाम (f)	bādām	almond
बाजरा (m)	bājara	millet
बाल (f)	bāl	ear
बाम मछली (f)	bām machhalī	eel
बार (m)	bār	pub, bar
बारमैन (m)	bāramain	bartender
बीफ़स्टीक (m)	bīfastīk	steak
बछड़े का गोश्त (m)	bachhare ka gosht	veal
बैंगन (m)	baingan	eggplant
बैरी (f)	bairī	waitress
बैरा (m)	baira	waiter
बर्च बोलेट (f)	barch bolet	birch bolete
बर्फ़ (m)	barf	ice
बर्फ़ के साथ	barf ke sāth	with ice
बत्तख़ (f)	battakh	duck
बेकन (m)	bekan	bacon

बेरी (f)	berī	berry
बेरियां (f pl)	beriyān	berries
भाग (m)	bhāg	portion
भूख (f)	bhūkh	appetite
भेड़ का गोश्त (m)	bher ka gosht	lamb
भुना	bhuna	fried
बिल (m)	bil	check
बिलबेरी (f)	bilaberī	bilberry
बिस्कुट (m)	biskut	cookies
बियर (m)	biyar	beer
ब्लैकबेरी (f)	blaikaberī	blackberry
बोतल ओपनर (m)	botal opanar	bottle opener
ब्रीम (f)	brīm	bream
ब्रसेल्स स्प्राउट्स (m)	brasels sprauts	Brussels sprouts
ब्रेड (f)	bred	bread
ब्रोकोली (f)	brokolī	broccoli
चावल (m)	chāval	rice
चाय (f)	chāy	tea
चीकू (m)	chīkū	kiwi
चीकन (m)	chīkan	chicken
चीनी (f)	chīnī	sugar
चूइन्ग गम (m)	chūing gam	chewing gum
चम्मच (m)	chammach	spoon
चम्मच (m)	chammach	teaspoon
चम्मच (m)	chammach	soup spoon
चटनी (f)	chatanī	sauce
छिलका (f)	chhilaka	peel
छुरी (f)	chhurī	knife
चिंगड़ा (m)	chingara	shrimp
चॉकलेट (m)	chokalet	chocolate
चॉकलेटी	chokaletī	chocolate
चुकन्दर (m)	chukandar	beetroot
दाल (m)	dāl	lentil
दालचीनी (f)	dālachīnī	cinnamon
दाना (m)	dāna	grain
डार्क बियर (m)	dārk biyar	dark beer
दूध (m)	dūdh	milk
दूध के साथ कॉफ़ी (f)	dūdh ke sāth kofī	coffee with milk
दही (m)	dahī	yogurt
डाइट (m)	dait	diet
दलिया (f)	daliya	porridge
डेथ कैप (f)	deth kaip	death cap
धनिया (m)	dhaniya	coriander
धुएँ में पकाया हुआ	dhuen men pakāya hua	smoked
डिब्बाबन्द खाना (m)	dibbāband khāna	canned food
दोपहर का भोजन (m)	dopahar ka bhojan	lunch
एपेरेतीफ़ (m)	eperetīf	aperitif
एपेटाइज़र (m)	epetaizar	appetizer
एस्पैरेगस (m)	espairegas	asparagus
एवोकाडो (m)	evokādo	avocado
फूल गोभी (f)	fūl gobhī	cauliflower
फल (m)	fal	fruit

फल (m pl)	fal	fruits
फली (f pl)	falī	beans
फ़िलिंग (f)	filing	filling
फ्लाई ऐगेरिक (f)	flaī aigerik	fly agaric
फ़्लैटफ़िश (f)	flaitafish	flatfish
फ्रोज़न	frozan	frozen
गाजर (f)	gājar	carrot
गाय का गोश्त (m)	gāy ka gosht	beef
गगन-धूलि (f)	gagan-dhūli	mushroom
गरम	garam	hot
गेहूं (m)	gehūn	wheat
गिलास (m)	gilās	glass
गोश्त (m)	gosht	meat
ग्रेपफ्रूट (m)	grepafrūt	grapefruit
हाथीचक (m)	hāthīchak	artichoke
हैलिबट (f)	hailibat	halibut
हैम (m)	haim	ham
हैमबर्गर (m)	haimabargar	hamburger
हल्का बियर (m)	halka biyar	light beer
हंस (m)	hans	goose
हरी चाय (f)	harī chāy	green tea
हरी सब्ज़ियाँ (f)	harī sabziyān	greens
हेरिंग मछली (f)	hering machhalī	herring
हेज़लनट (m)	hezalanat	hazelnut
इन्सटेन्ट-काफ़ी (f)	insatent-kāfī	instant coffee
जीभ (m)	jībh	tongue
जई (f)	jaī	oats
जैम (m)	jaim	jam
जैम (m)	jaim	jam
जैतून (m)	jaitūn	olives
जैतून का तेल (m)	jaitūn ka tel	olive oil
जंगली स्ट्रॉबेरी (f)	jangalī stroberī	wild strawberry
जौ (m)	jau	barley
जिगर (f)	jigar	liver
जिन (f)	jin	gin
काली चाय (f)	kālī chāy	black tea
काली किशमिश (f)	kālī kishamish	blackcurrant
काली कॉफ़ी (f)	kālī kofī	black coffee
काली मिर्च (f)	kālī mirch	black pepper
काँटा (m)	kānta	fork
काबौहाइड्रेट (m)	kārbohaidret	carbohydrates
काबौनेटेड	kārboneted	carbonated
कार्प (f)	kārp	carp
कीमा (m)	kīma	hamburger
कद्दू	kaddū	pumpkin
कैलोरी (f)	kailorī	calorie
कैपूचिनो (f)	kaipūchino	cappuccino
कैटफ़िश (f)	kaitafish	catfish
काओबेरी (f)	kaoberī	cowberry
कड़वा	karava	bitter
केक (m)	kek	cake
केकड़ा (m)	kekara	crab

केला (m)	kela	banana
खाना (m)	khāna	food
खाने योग्य गगन-धूलि (f)	khāne yogy gagan-dhūli	edible mushroom
खीरा (m)	khīra	cucumber
खूबानी (f)	khūbānī	apricot
खजूर (m)	khajūr	date
खरबूजा (f)	kharabūza	melon
खरगोश (m)	kharagosh	rabbit
खट्टी क्रीम (f)	khattī krīm	sour cream
किशमिश (m)	kishamish	raisin
कॉड (f)	kod	cod
कॉफ़ी (f)	kofī	coffee
कॉकटेल (m)	kokatel	cocktail
कोल्ड ड्रिंक (f)	kold drink	soft drink
कोन्याक (m)	konyāk	cognac
कॉर्नफ्लेक्स (m)	kornafleks	cornflakes
क्रीम (m)	krīm	buttercream
क्रेनबेरी (f)	krenaberī	cranberry
लाल किशमिश (f)	lāl kishamish	redcurrant
लाल मिर्च (m)	lāl mirch	red pepper
लाल शिमला मिर्च पाउडर (m)	lāl shimala mirch paudar	paprika
लाल वाइन (f)	lāl vain	red wine
लहसुन (m)	lahasun	garlic
लौंग (f)	laung	cloves
लेमोनेड (m)	lemoned	lemonade
लिकर (m)	likar	liqueur
लोबस्टर (m)	lobastar	spiny lobster
माक्रैल (f)	mākrail	mackerel
मीठा	mītha	sweet
मीठा (m)	mītha	dessert
मूली (f)	mūlī	radish
मूंगफली (m)	mūngafalī	peanut
मछली (f)	machhalī	fish
मछली के अंडे (m)	machhalī ke ande	caviar
मकई (f)	makī	corn
मक्का (m)	makka	corn
मक्खन (m)	makkhan	butter
मलाई (f pl)	malaī	cream
मसाला (m)	masāla	condiment
मसाला (m)	masāla	spice
मटर (m)	matar	pea
मेनू (m)	menū	menu
मेयोनेज़ (m)	meyonez	mayonnaise
मिल्कशेक (m)	milkashek	milkshake
मिनरल वॉटर (m)	minaral votar	mineral water
मिठाई (f pl)	mithaī	confectionery
मोरेल (f)	morel	morel
मोथी (m)	mothī	buckwheat
मुरब्बा (m)	murabba	marmalade
नारंगी (m)	nārangī	mandarin
नारंगी छतरी वाली गगन-धूलि (f)	nārangī chhatarī vālī gagan-dhūli	orange-cap boletus

नारियल (m)	nāriyal	coconut
नाशपाती (f)	nāshapātī	pear
नाश्ता (m)	nāshta	breakfast
नींबू (m)	nīmbū	lemon
नूडल्स (m)	nūdals	noodles
नकली मक्खन (m)	nakalī makkhan	margarine
नमक (m)	namak	salt
नमकीन	namakīn	salty
ओपनर (m)	opanar	can opener
पालक (m)	pālak	spinach
पानी (m)	pānī	water
पास्ता (m)	pāsta	pasta
पीने का पानी (f)	pīne ka pānī	drinking water
पीट्ज़ा (f)	pītza	pizza
पाई (m)	paī	pie
पाइक (f)	paik	pike
पाइक पर्च (f)	paik parch	pike perch
पकवान (m)	pakavān	course, dish
पनीर (m)	panīr	cheese
पपीता (f)	papīta	papaya
पर्च (f)	parch	perch
पत्ता गोभी (f)	patta gobhī	cabbage
पेंचकस (m)	penchakas	corkscrew
पेस्ट्री (f)	pestrī	cake
पिसा हुआ गोश्त (m)	pisa hua gosht	pâté
पिस्ता (m)	pista	pistachios
प्रोटीन (m pl)	protīn	proteins
प्याला (m)	pyāla	cup
प्याज़ (m)	pyāz	onion
राजमा (f)	rājama	kidney bean
रात्रिभोज (m)	rātribhoj	dinner
रई (f)	raī	rye
रबड़ी (f)	rabarī	condensed milk
रैसीपी (f)	raisīpī	recipe
रम (m)	ram	rum
रस (m)	ras	juice
रसभरी (f)	rasabharī	raspberry
रसुला (f)	rasula	russula
सालमन (m)	sālaman	salmon
सार्डीन (f)	sārdīn	sardine
सीप (m)	sīp	oyster
सूखा	sūkha	dried
सूप (m)	sūp	soup
सूरजमुखी तेल (m)	sūrajamukhī tel	sunflower oil
सब्ज़ियाँ (f pl)	sabziyān	vegetables
सफ़ेद गगन-धूलि (f)	safed gagan-dhūli	cep
सफ़ेद वाइन (f)	safed vain	white wine
साइड डिश (f)	said dish	side dish
सैन्डविच (m)	saindavich	sandwich
सलाद (m)	salād	salad
सलाद पत्ता (m)	salād patta	lettuce
समुद्री खाना (m)	samudrī khāna	seafood

संतरा (m)	santara	orange
संतरे का रस (m)	santare ka ras	orange juice
सरसों (m)	sarason	mustard
सौंफ़ (f)	saumf	anise
सेब (m)	seb	apple
सेलरी (m)	selarī	celery
शाकाहारी (m)	shākāhārī	vegetarian
शाकाहारी	shākāhārī	vegetarian
शार्क (f)	shārk	shark
शीतलक ड्रिंक (f)	shītalak drink	refreshing drink
शहद (m)	shahad	honey
शैम्पेन (f)	shaimpen	champagne
शलजम (f)	shalajam	turnip
शराब (m pl)	sharāb	liquors
शराब रहित	sharāb rahit	non-alcoholic
शैंटरेल (f)	shentarel	chanterelle
शिकार के पशुपक्षी (f)	shikār ke pashupakshī	game
शिमला मिर्च (m)	shimala mirch	bell pepper
सिरका (m)	siraka	vinegar
स्कीड (m)	skīd	squid
सोआ (m)	soa	dill
सॉसर (m)	sosar	saucer
सॉसेज (f)	sosej	sausage
सोया (m)	soya	soy
स्पार्कलिंग	spārkaling	sparkling
स्पेघेटी (f)	speghetī	spaghetti
स्टर्जन (f)	starjan	sturgeon
स्टिल वॉटर	stil votar	still
स्ट्रॉबेरी (f)	stroberī	strawberry
सुअर की जांघ (f)	suar kī jāngh	gammon
सुअर का गोश्त (m)	suar ka gosht	pork
स्वाद (m)	svād	taste, flavor
स्वाद (m)	svād	aftertaste
स्वादिष्ट	svādisht	tasty
ताज़ा रस (m)	tāza ras	freshly squeezed juice
टूना (f)	tūna	tuna
टूथपिक (m)	tūthapik	toothpick
टमाटर (m)	tamātar	tomato
टमाटर का रस (m)	tamātar ka ras	tomato juice
तरबूज़ (m)	tarabūz	watermelon
टर्की (m)	tarkī	turkey
तश्तरी (f)	tashtarī	plate
तेजपत्ता (m)	tejapatta	bay leaf
तेल (m)	tel	vegetable oil
ठंडा	thanda	cold
तिल (m)	til	sesame
टिप (f)	tip	tip
टॉफ़ी (f)	tofī	candy
ट्राउट मछली (f)	traut machhalī	trout
टुकड़ा (m)	tukara	slice
टुकड़ा (m)	tukara	piece
टुकड़ा (m)	tukara	crumb

तुलसी (f)	tulasī	basil
तुरई (f)	turī	zucchini
उबला	ubala	boiled
वाइन (f)	vain	wine
वाइन गिलास (m)	vain gilās	glass
वाइन सूची (f)	vain sūchī	wine list
वर्मोउथ (f)	varmauth	vermouth
वसा (m pl)	vasa	fats
वेफ्रर (m pl)	vefar	waffles
विस्की (f)	viskī	whiskey
विटामिन (m)	vitāmin	vitamin
वियना सॉसेज (m)	viyana sosej	vienna sausage
वोड़का (m)	vodaka	vodka
व्यंजन (m)	vyanjan	cuisine
यख़नी (f)	yakhanī	clear soup
ज़ाफ्रान (m)	zāfarān	saffron
ज़ीरा (m)	zīra	caraway
ज़हरीली गगन-धूलि (f)	zaharīlī gagan-dhūli	poisonous mushroom